NEW MERMAIDS

General editor: Brian Gibbons
Professor of English Literature, University of Münster

The interior of a Restoration theatre
drawn by C. Walter Hodges

NEW MERMAIDS

NEW MERMAIDS

GEORGE FARQUHAR

THE BEAUX' STRATAGEM

edited by Ann Blake
Formerly Senior Lecturer in English
La Trobe University, Melbourne

Bloomsbury Methuen Drama
An imprint of Bloomsbury Publishing Plc

B L O O M S B U R Y
LONDON • NEW DELHI • NEW YORK • SYDNEY

Bloomsbury Methuen Drama

An imprint of Bloomsbury Publishing Plc

Imprint previously known as Methuen Drama

50 Bedford Square   1385 Broadway
London   New York
WC1B 3DP   NY 10018
UK   USA

www.bloomsbury.com

**BLOOMSBURY, METHUEN DRAMA and the Diana logo are trademarks of
Bloomsbury Publishing Plc**

Second edition 2006 first published by A&C Black Publishers Ltd
Reprinted by Bloomsbury Methuen Drama 2015

First edition 1988

© 2006 A&C Black Publishers Ltd

British Library Cataloguing-in-Publication Data
A catalogue record for this book is available from the British Library.

ISBN: PB: 978-0-7136-7000-4
ePDF: 978-1-4081-4427-5
ePub: 978-1-4081-4428-2

Library of Congress Cataloging-in-Publication Data
A catalog record for this book is available from the Library of Congress.

Series: New Mermaids

CONTENTS

ACKNOWLEDGEMENTS

In preparing this edition my principal debts are to the previous New Mermaid editor, Michael Cordner, and to Shirley Strum Kenny, editor of the standard edition of Farquhar's works. Other editors to whose work I am indebted, along with the writers of biographical and critical studies of Farquhar, I have endeavoured to acknowledge in the footnotes and in the Further Reading. I am grateful to the Bodleian Library, the University of Oxford, for permission to use as copy text a copy of the first edition (Mal. 138(7)), and to reproduce its title page. William Hodges and the library staff were always helpful with my long distance enquiries, and on my visits. I owe particular thanks to Charles Edelman for replying so promptly to a request for advice, to Anne Margaret Daniel at Princeton for drawing my attention to *The Belle's Stratagem*, and to my old friends Jo and George Watson for conversations about Ireland and Irish writers. Jenny Ridout and Katie Taylor at A & C Black have been unfailingly helpful at all stages of the production of this edition. Thanks finally to Sue Gibbons, my copy editor, for her careful work, to Brian Gibbons, the series' General Editor, for his amiable guidance, and to Derick Marsh, for his constant support, advice and criticism. Any remaining errors are my own.

Melbourne, 2005   A. B.

INTRODUCTION

The Author

George Farquhar was born in 1677 or 1678 in Derry, in the north of Ireland, the son of 'an eminent divine of ye Church of England'. As such the Reverend Farquhar was a target for Catholic resentment and attack, and he is reported to have been 'plundered and burnt out of all that he had . . . and after dy'd with greif'.[1] Conflict between Protestant and Catholic came close to Farquhar again in 1689 when Derry stood out against James II's army, and endured siege and starvation. A year later Farquhar was, it is claimed, a volunteer at the Battle of the Boyne,[2] and in an early poem he commemorated the death of the Protestant commander of this victory over Catholic forces. Farquhar entered Trinity College Dublin on 17 July 1694, aged seventeen, as a sizar – a student performing menial duties in return for an allowance. In 1695 he was awarded a scholarship worth four pounds a year but lost it through bad behaviour. By 1696, according to accounts of his life published in eighteenth-century editions of his plays,[3] he had left college, rejecting what he was to call 'the rigidness of teachers, and pedantry of schools',[4] and taken up acting at the Smock Alley theatre in Dublin, beginning, surprisingly, with Othello. As an actor, it is reported, he had no voice, though 'a very good person', and besides, luck was against him: in a performance of Dryden's *The Indian Emperor*, he accidentally wounded a fellow actor and vowed to give up acting for ever. In 1698, probably at the suggestion of the Irish actor Robert Wilks, who had already performed in London, he moved to London, and began to write for the stage. In the years between 1698 and his early death in 1707 he produced seven comedies, three of them not well received, but three others, *The Constant Couple* (1699) and his last two, *The Recruiting Officer* and *The Beaux' Stratagem*, all immediate successes and among the most popular plays of the century, as was his one afterpiece, *The Stage-Coach*. He also published *Love and Business*, a collection of poems, letters, and a prose

---

1 According to Farquhar's widow, in a petition for a pension to Queen Anne, 1709; see James R. Sutherland, 'New Light on George Farquhar', *TLS*, 6 March 1937, p. 171.
2 Again, according to Margaret Farquhar's petition.
3 The first by W. R. Chetwood, assisted by Robert Wilks, appeared in 1728; Thomas Wilkes compiled a lengthier version for *The Works of George Farquhar* (Dublin 1775).
4 *The Constant Couple*, I.i.131–3; Vizard is speaking in praise of the hero, Sir Harry Wildair: 'has had a genteel and easy Education, free from the rigidness', etc.

piece responding to Jeremy Collier's recent attack on the indecency of the stage, and contributed to three other miscellanies of this kind. For the theatre he produced prologues and epilogues, including one for the return of Wilks to the London stage (1699), but, as Kenny notes, this Irish playwright was never a member of any theatrical group, or literary circle.

After his lack of stage success, Farquhar became a soldier. He had a wife and family to provide for. He married Margaret Pemell, probably in 1703, a widow with three children. The early Lives tell a romantic, but possibly unreliable, story: 'For his wife (by whom he had two daughters only) through the reputation of a great fortune, tricked him into matrimony. This was chiefly the fault of her love, which was so violent for him, that she resolved to leave nothing untried to gain him.' To his 'immortal honour' he forgave her.[5] Nevertheless many writers assume the marriage must have been unhappy. Among the few known facts of Farquhar's life are the records of his brief military career. These establish that in 1704 Farquhar was commissioned as a lieutenant in a new regiment raised by an Irish peer, the Duke of Ormond, and commanded by the Earl of Orrery.[6] He was engaged in two periods of recruiting, in Shrewsbury and, probably, Lichfield, separated by a period in mid 1705 when the regiment was in Ireland, and where, the early Lives relate, he acted Sir Harry Wildair for Ormond, then Lord Lieutenant of Ireland, at Dublin Castle. Again, it is said, his acting let him down, but he received a hundred pounds. As for making money from his military career, recruiting left him out of pocket, as his commander admitted.[7] To pay his debts, according to the early Lives, he sold his commission, and did so encouraged by Ormond's promise of a post of captain. None was forthcoming. He turned back to the stage: and though *The Recruiting Officer* was a phenomenal success, his situation grew more and more desperate. Finally, with money and encouragement from Wilks, he wrote *The Beaux' Stratagem*, but, broken by illness and worry, died in London, and was buried on 23 May 1707.[8]

Given the lack of personal reminiscences of Farquhar by his con-

---

5   1728; in her petition Margaret Farquhar makes it clear that she had lost her fortune
    before the death of her first husband.
6   Robert John Jordan, 'George Farquhar's Military Career', *Huntington Library Quarterly*,
    37 (1974), 251–64.
7   See the Earl of Orrery's 'certificate' supporting Mrs Farquhar's petition, Sutherland,
    op. cit.
8   Eric Rothstein, *George Farquhar* (NY 1967), p. 29 records that the burial register spells
    him 'Falkwere' reflecting, Rothstein suggests, a Derry pronunciation.

temporaries,[9] it is more than usually tempting to look for the writer in his work. He teasingly suggests this tactic himself in his first play *Love and a Bottle* where Lyric, a poor writer, declares that 'the hero in comedy is always the poet's character'.[10] The description of Wildair, 'An airy gentleman affecting humourous gaiety and freedom in his behaviour' makes it obvious what qualities Farquhar admired – and perhaps possessed.[11] Among the published love-letters is a self-portrait. What he writes there of his lack of 'estate' and his capacity to write quickly and earn money takes the reader momentarily close to the tough circumstances of his short life, and the humour with which he countered them: 'I have very little estate, but what lies under the circumference of my hat ... but I ought to thank providence that I can by three hours study live one and twenty with satisfaction myself, and contribute to the maintenance of more families than some who have thousands a year.'[12]

In his plays, as in his prefaces and dedications, his boldness, inventiveness, wit and independence shine out. His 1775 biographer however concluded on a note of pathos. One may see Farquhar's disposition best, he wrote, in 'that very laconic but expressive billet which Mr Wilkes [Wilks, the actor] found after his death, among his papers, directed to him ... "Dear Bob, I have not anything to leave thee to perpetuate my memory, but these two helpless girls; look upon them sometimes, and think of him that was, to the last moment of his life, thine, GEORGE FARQUHAR" '. According to the 1728 Life, the dying Farquhar flung all his papers into the fire, and so this note, like other anecdotes, remains uncorroborated. His comedies are his lasting legacy. They have a secure place among what, in his 'Discourse upon Comedy', he called 'the darlings of the English audience'.[13]

The Play

The Beaux' Stratagem, Farquhar's last play, was written when he was dying. He lived long enough to know it was an immediate success and it went on to become one of the most performed plays of the eighteenth century. Farquhar's warm-hearted humour, vitality and wit light up the play, as they did his own last days, according to reports. For instance,

9 In *An Apology for the Life of Colley Cibber* Cibber refers to Farquhar's plays and the great acting roles he created, but tells no stories of him; he attributes the 'discovery' of Anne Oldfield not to Farquhar in the first place and then to Vanbrugh but to Vanbrugh alone.
10 *Love and a Bottle*, IV.ii.47–8.
11 Description of Sir Harry Wildair in the Dramatis Personae, *The Constant Couple*.
12 Kenny, II, 352.
13 Kenny, II, 380.

when the actress Anne Oldfield complained that he had given her character Mrs Sullen to Archer 'without a proper divorce, which was not a security for her honour . . . "to salve this," replied our author, "I'll get a real divorce, marry her myself, and give her my bond she shall be a real widow in less than a fortnight." '[14]

The plot follows the familiar outline mocked by the hack writer Lyric in Farquhar's *Love and a Bottle*: the gentleman-rake hero bears off the great fortune, and all ends in marriage.[15] But here the race for sex and money has the gentle tone of that 'humane comedy' (in Kenny's phrase)[16] which evolved during the 1690s. The satire is more genial, and there is less of the 'immorality and profaneness' condemned by Collier in his 1698 attack on the stage. Though Mrs Sullen comes teasingly close to sexual impropriety, none occurs. Everyone still speaks frankly about sex, and the men talk with rakish determination about getting hold of money, but then sentiment breaks in, and finer feelings emerge. The treatment of the comic butts, Scrub and Foigard, is sympathetic, not destructive.

The country setting of *The Beaux' Stratagem*, and of Farquhar's preceding play, *The Recruiting Officer*, rare in comedies of this time, gives both plays a distinctive freshness. Mrs Sullen may despise 'country pleasures', but rural characters here are valued as well as teased. The comedy's moments of concern with serious human situations, particularly poverty and marriage, are another aspect of its distinctive appeal. Though obtaining a divorce is today relatively straightforward, the lines about compatibility in marriage still resonate. And with these concerns comes a greater psychological complexity of characterization – in the unhappy Mrs Sullen, and in Archer's resentment of his poverty, and arguably in the miserable Squire Sullen. Mrs Sullen and Archer are roles worthy of great actors, and the 'minor persons . . . invested with a distinction almost Shakespearean',[17] have proved equally attractive to actors, and to audiences. It is the play's capturing of this range and depth of characters, and its refusal to patronize any one of them that is so remarkable. It not only anticipates the later comedy of Sheridan and Goldsmith, a point often made, but also forges links with the comedy of the past.

14 A much repeated anecdote, quoted here from Thomas Wilkes' 'Life', cited in Kenny, II, 133 (substituting 'honour' for husband in agreement with other accounts).
15 See IV.ii. 50–4.
16 Shirley Strum Kenny, 'Humane Comedy', *Modern Philology*, 75 (1977–8), 24–43.
17 Louis A. Strauss, *A Discourse upon Comedy*: '*The Recruiting Officer* and *The Beaux' Stratagem* (Boston, 1914), reprinted in Raymond A. Anselment, ed., *The Recruiting Officer and The Beaux' Stratagem: a Casebook* (Basingstoke 1977), p. 63.

Dorinda (Jane Gurnett) and Lady Bountiful (Matyelok Gibbs) revive Ainwell (Paul Mooney) (IV.i) in Peter Wood's National Theatre Production, 1989. © Clive Barda/ArenaPAL

Farquhar was an inventive, even experimental writer. He evolved as a playwright, as indeed did 'Restoration comedy', in the years from 1660 to 1735. In this play he combines a recognizably Restoration plot turning on the fortune-hunting of a contrasting pair of pleasure-loving rakes with a more late-Restoration theme, marital discord. *The Beaux' Stratagem*'s bedroom seduction scene has a parallel in Vanbrugh's *The Relapse* (1700), and the unhappily matched Sullens recall Sir John and Lady Brute in Vanbrugh's *The Provoked Wife*.[18] A favourite scene in Restoration comedy, the proviso scene, where a couple negotiates a marriage, most famously in *The Way of the World*, appears in a variation when the Sullens arrange not a marriage but a divorce. But Farquhar's management of these materials has a respect for kinder feeling, which, for all his Restoration vitality, distinguishes him from his late-Restoration contemporary, Vanbrugh.

The comedies of the 1680s and 90s pay more attention to marriage and its problems, and less to courtship. This new emphasis can be attributed in part to the expectations of an audience now less rakish, more middle-class, and especially to 'the ladies', then equated with its moral element. Demands for reform of the stage culminated in Collier's 1698 denunciation of playwrights, for 'their smuttiness of expression; their swearing, profaneness, and lewd application of Scripture; their abuse of the clergy; their making their top characters libertines, and giving them success in their debauchery'. Though impatient of Collier's attack, Farquhar felt its influence, wryly noting in his Preface to *The Constant Couple* (1699), 'I have not displeased the ladies, nor offended the clergy'. In *The Beaux Stratagem*, 'humane comedy' is most obvious when Aimwell becomes a figure of sentiment, so moved by love for Dorinda that he can no longer deceive her. His reformation is believably human, just as is Plume's when, in *The Recruiting Officer*, he gives up his life of liberty for marriage. Farquhar prepares us for this change with Archer's earlier complaint about his friend's 'romantic airs' (III.ii.15). Archer keeps *his* eye on feeding his needs for sex and money without emotional entanglement. Or does he? One of the great attractions of the comedy is the intriguing development of the relationship between Archer and Mrs Sullen. The humanity of the late Farquhar is apparent throughout the serio-comic miseries of Mrs Sullen, neither unwaveringly chaste like Vanbrugh's Amanda, nor willingly seduced like his Berinthia. In a telling difference, Archer's attempt to possess the lady is interrupted, but

---

18 Colley Cibber's *The Lady's Last Stake* (December 1707) imitates Farquhar's Sullens in Lord and Lady Wronglove's discussions of separating.

his scenes with Mrs Sullen captivate with their own sexual excitement as he presses her, and she struggles between her scruples and inclinations.

In constructing this comedy Farquhar has produced a less complex intrigue, and abandoned one of his favoured devices, the cross-dressed heroine, thereby reducing the opportunities for sexual innuendo. In comparison to his earlier comedies, the incidents are less contrived, the characters less exaggerated, and, critics agree, more 'natural'.[19] Nevertheless, Farquhar provides the diverse incidents and neatly interwoven subplots which, contrary to neoclassical rules of unity of action, he believed the playwright should devise to entertain his audience.[20] The scene in Mrs Sullen's bedroom is, as Styan claims, a masterpiece of comic writing. The inventive sequence of events, all carefully indicated in the stage directions, deftly brings the plots together. Archer's appearance from the closet, though anticipated since the audience knows his plan to hide there instead of the Count (IV.ii.100–1), is a dramatic surprise when it actually happens. It leads into Mrs Sullen's wavering and that is ended only by the arrival of Scrub. His comic terror, mistaking Archer for a thief, 'take all we have', and his hiding behind the bed with his 'dear brother' Martin, provide a nice contrast to Gibbet's equally comic self-possession, before and after his capture: 'Sir, I'll have no prayer at all; the government has provided a chaplain to say prayers for us on these occasions' (V.ii.143–4).

The range of characters in this play is another striking feature, and one it shares with *The Recruiting Officer*. Where the action in that play moves about the town of Shrewsbury, here it moves between Lady Bountiful's house, and a Lichfield inn. Farquhar had previously, in collaboration with Peter Motteux, written a play set in an inn, the highly successful afterpiece, *The Stage-Coach*.[21] The adventures of Don Quixote, and dramatic versions of them,[22] perhaps also contributed to the choice of setting. Besides these literary promptings, it is not wholly impossible that, as a plaque on the George Inn in Lichfield proclaims, Farquhar

19 So much so that the names of two characters, Lady Bountiful and Bonniface, went into the language meaning benevolent country lady, and jovial host.
20 See 'A Discourse upon Comedy', Kenny, II, pp. 367–8 and p. 382.
21 First performed between autumn 1700 and February 1702, and based on *Les Carrosses d'Orléans* by Jean de la Chapelle. For the suggestion that Farquhar wrote all but the song, see Shirley Strum Kenny, 'The Mystery of Farquhar's *The Stage-Coach* Reconsidered', *Studies in Bibliography*, 32 (1979), 219–36.
22 For Thomas Durfey's popular '*Comical History of Don Quixote*' (1694–5) and other Quixote plays see Gordon K. Thomas, 'The Knight among the Dunces', *Restoration and Eighteenth-Century Theatre Research*, 14 (1975), 10–22, 11–13, and the note at II.ii.219–20.

wrote his play there. Using a location where people of all ranks in society are brought together in one place, as in a stage-coach: 'Here chance kindly mixes, / All sorts and all sexes' (Kenny, I, 324–5), now seems unremarkable, but then it was not. Humble people in Restoration comedy do not have major roles, but here they are at least both prominent and sympathetically presented.[23] *The Stage-Coach* is a miniature version of *The Beaux' Stratagem* as farce, with its heroine fleeing an arranged marriage, her booby fiancé, her lover, the comic Irish servant, and the coachman pursuing the maid Dolly from bedroom to bedroom. In the full-length play, Farquhar develops romantic and marriage plots, weaves in a burglary plot, and still has space to develop the innkeeper and Cherry the maid, and to flesh out the highwayman, Gibbet. Gibbet's professional style of managing his business endears him to the audience. But it was Scrub, in his lowly station, who became the audience's favourite, and one of the best loved comic roles of the eighteenth century. Like so many of the figures in the play he is a life-like mixture. Some have complained his Latin phrases do not suit a country factotum, but they are commonplace phrases, and surely acceptable in one who can mimic '*the French air*' and throw the occasional innuendo to Mrs Sullen (III.i.89–90). He is not easy to sum up, his 'world of simplicity', as Dorinda points out, often masking a cunning sense of what's going on (III.i.71). Moving between the Inn and Lady Bountiful's are Foigard, the Irish priest masquerading as a native of Brussels who plots with the ladies' maid, Gipsy, and Count Bellair, who courts Mrs Sullen. Foigard, the last in a line of Farquhar's comic Irishmen, is the most engaging, and the most pretentious. Like Gibbet, he is uncrushable. The Count, a French prisoner, contributes to the play's topicality. Like the numerous military metaphors which all through the play colour the speech of men and women alike, the Count is an acknowledgement of the war proceeding outside the play. Though the play indulges the audience's patriotism in a few lines of anti-French and anti-Catholic feeling, the figure of the Count redresses the balance. His debonair response to Mrs Sullen's manipulation of his courtship, his 'French air', is admirable. Nevertheless, according to the 1728 edition, the role of the Count was 'cut out by the author, after the first night's representation.' Mrs Sullen's manipulation of him detracts from the interplay between her and Archer, and the comedy can bear losing him.

23 John Loftis, *Comedy and Society from Congreve to Fielding* (Stanford 1959), pp. 48–9.

TOWN AND COUNTRY

Everyone writing about Farquhar remarks that in his two last plays a new freshness comes with their country settings. Leigh Hunt, writing in 1840 on *The Recruiting Officer*, 'We seem to breathe the clear fresh ruddy-making air of a remote country town',[24] has been echoed repeatedly in remarks on the play's 'sunny country air'.[25] In *The Recruiting Officer* there is a move outdoors into the Herefordshire countryside, with two scenes set on 'The Walk by the Severn side'. From the opening in the Market Place where Sergeant Kite addresses the 'Mob' of local people, a sense of a country town and its surroundings builds up, with the recruits Coster Pearmain and Thomas Appletree, and Rose who comes to town to sell her chickens with her brother Bullock, all of them part of a community presided over by the admirable Justice Balance, Farquhar's own version of Justice Shallow, younger, patriotic, and an indulgent father.

In *The Beaux' Stratagem* the sense of an outside London 'freshness' emerges more subtly. The scenes are 'in and about Lichfield' (I.i.67–8) but all are indoors: at the Inn or Lady Bountiful's house. Nevertheless, innumerable points of detail suggest a distinctively provincial setting: from Bonniface's remark about Lichfield being an 'inland town, and indifferently provided with fish' (I.i.238–9), to Mrs Sullen's satirical picture of 'country pleasures' and 'rural accomplishments', and Archer's remarks describing the approach to Lady Bountiful's house: 'drawn by the appearance of your handsome house to view it nearer, and walking up the avenue within five paces of the courtyard' (IV.i.70–2).

But rather than the physical location it is the inhabitants who most create a sense of 'not London'. Lady Bountiful, Dorinda, Squire Sullen, Bonniface, Cherry, Scrub, Gipsy and the country-woman who comes seeking a cure for her husband's bad leg, all contribute to it in various ways. At the simplest level is the naive country-woman who, in perhaps the play's oldest joke, innocently suggests her husband is reluctant to work: 'No, no, madam, the poor man's inclinable enough to lie still' (IV.i.51). A more complex type is Bonniface, the self-assured, cheery innkeeper, 'Mr Guts', who lives on his own ale, has his own 'fraternity' of highwaymen, and is willing to prostitute his daughter. Jovial and outrageous, cunning but easily imposed on, he embodies the play's 'tone of healthy vitality and of easy accommodation to evil'.[26] Squire Sullen

24 *The Dramatic Works of Wycherley, Congreve, Vanbrugh and Farquhar*, with Biographical and Critical Notices by Leigh Hunt, [1840] (London 1849), p. 18.

25 Robert D. Hume, *The Rakish Stage: Studies in English Drama, 1660–1800* (Carbondale 1983), p. 227.

26 Loftis, *Comedy and Society*, p. 72.

'Captain' Gibbet (Paul Curran) fails to convince Aimwell (Ronald Pickup) (III.ii).

Bonniface (Gerald James) and Cherry (Helen Frazer) are puzzled by Aimwell's box 'full of money' (I.i).
Both pictures from National Theatre production, 1970, © Douglas Jeffery

with his 'good parcel of land' and his assorted unrefined drinking companions, 'the constable ... the exciseman, the hunchbacked barber' (V.i.10–11), the least attractive of the country folk, is no caricature rustic, as his conversation with Sir Charles in Act V.i makes clear. As for Lady Bountiful and Dorinda, the 'country ladies' as Mrs Sullen thinks of them, they are marked by their directness and vigour. Lady Bountiful is a new kind of old lady in English comedy, still laughable, but also benevolent. She takes pride in her knowledge of herbs and distilling, her wholesome country remedies prevailing when, as Bonniface asserts, London trained doctors do only harm. Though her determination to minister to Aimwell is made fun of in IV.i when she is imposed on by the young men, the efficacy of her good works is in no doubt. Her servant Scrub tells us most about living in the country as he complains about his weekly round of duties. He like the rest of the country figures is deceived by 'Martin', but, as just noted, his naivety masks a country cunning of his own. He also possesses a coward's ability to save his own skin, always a good source of comedy. Gipsy, in her dealings with Foigard, displays a false naiveté: she is another very well able to look after herself. The presentation of these figures achieves a remarkable solidity. Farquhar's affectionate treatment of them is far from either the traditional celebration of country innocence, or London scorn of rustic uncouthness.

More in accord with most Restoration comedy, the play's city folk praise the pleasures of London and bemoan the lack of anything like them in the country. 'O London, London,' rhapsodize Archer and Aimwell. Only lack of money has dragged them down to the country. Mrs Sullen thinks of her unhappiness in terms of her distaste for 'country pleasures', as well as for her Squire husband. At different moments, Cherry, Gibbet and Dorinda all look forward to leaving the country for a high life in London. Nevertheless, the play radiates a sense of the Lichfield people living in their own style without any sense of inferiority when, for instance Bonniface boasts of his ale, or praises the good works of Lady Bountiful, or Scrub talks about ploughing, hunting or dunning the tenants, or about Foigard and Gipsy 'devouring my lady's marmalade in the closet'. None of this is diminished by talk of London. The country folk stand on their own.

In giving his last two plays a country setting Farquhar took an unusual step. As Hume points out, only six of the seventy comedies written between 1660 and 1708 and set in England move out of London.[27] One is

27 Robert D. Hume, *The Development of English Drama in the late Seventeenth Century* (Oxford 1976), p. 140. Fifteen of the 85 comedies written between 1661 and 1709 have foreign settings (p. 139).

Vanbrugh's *The Country House* which turns on the idea of the house being mistaken for an inn, as in *She Stoops to Conquer*, with the owner being driven mad by his 'guests'. Another is *The Relapse* where some scenes are set at Sir Tunbelly's house. But here all is rustic uncouthness. Country locations in these few comedies, apart from Farquhar's, 'serve primarily as pretexts for sniping at rural life'.[28]

How far Farquhar was from sniping is apparent in his Epistle Dedicatory to *The Recruiting Officer*, addressed, significantly, to 'All Friends round the Wrekin', where, confident in his ability to create attractive but unidealized country people, he promises 'no person of any character in your county should suffer by being exposed'. This is at odds with most Restoration comedy, where what is not London is despicable, even horrific. A typical estimate is that of Millamant in *The Way of the World*, commenting on her cousin Sir Wilful Witwoud up from the country to woo her: 'Ah rustic! Ruder than Gothic' (IV.i.90). In his earlier comedies Farquhar could himself jibe at rural life, but that changed. The contrast between Dorinda, heiress to ten thousand pounds, and Miss Hoyden, the 'great fortune', daughter to Sir Tunbelly, wooed in Vanbrugh's *The Relapse* illustrates Farquhar's distinctive attitude. Where Dorinda is a country girl of sense and sensibility Miss Hoyden is ignorant, amoral and the occasion of much broad sexual comedy. Dorinda, though bowled over by Aimwell, observes her brother's marriage with clear eyes. In according respect to country figures of various ranks, when creating Bonniface, Scrub, and the charming Cherry, all dramatic successes, Farquhar went his own way, leaving others to debate the superiority of town or country.

CLASS, MONEY AND FORTUNE HUNTING:
'BECAUSE THEY WANTED MONEY' (II.i.37)

In Farquhar's time and on into the nineteenth century the recognized way for men and women of the upper, non-working classes to alter their social status was through marriage.[29] Love affairs among gentle folk were inevitably entangled with economic considerations, as readers of Jane Austen's novels learn. The opportunities offered by marriage could be vital for a young man, dependent, like Orlando in *As You Like It*, on the generosity of his elder brother. For the playwright, the situation of the younger brother, or indeed of any young man in search of a rich wife, is good dramatic material. Fortune hunters propel the plots of much

28 Loftis, *Comedy and Society*, p. 75.
29 Loftis, *Comedy and Society*, p. 45.

seventeenth-century comedy, from the city comedies of Middleton and others, to those of Vanbrugh and Farquhar. At the beginning of the play Aimwell, like the penniless Young Fashion in Vanbrugh's *The Relapse*, goes off to the country to marry riches. Aimwell and Archer, also a younger brother if what he tells Cherry is to be believed (II.ii.186), have between them spent one thousand pounds on the pleasures of London, and would do so again: they have not 'spent' their fortunes, they have 'enjoyed them'. Rejoicing in their energy and resourcefulness, they set out to mend their broken fortunes by establishing Aimwell as a wealthy lord, and using his brother's title: 'he would never give me anything else' (III.ii.57).

They are not the only ones in the play seeking to do just that: Gibbet and his gang plan a more direct attack on the riches of Lady Bountiful's house. Gibbet presents himself as a genteel thief who treats ladies with 'profound respect'. His ambition is to buy a place in the royal household and retire. Ever the gentleman-highwayman (already at this time a recognized type), he excuses his way of life: he too is 'only a younger brother' (V.ii.123). The parallel between the two schemes encouraged commentators (Roper and others) to see each reinforcing condemnation of the other: the young men are no better than the professional thieves. Indeed Kenneth Muir, in a facetious comment on those who deplore the sexual immorality of Restoration comedy, insists that the beaux' stratagem is more reprehensible than anything planned by Valentine or Mirabell.[30] But to condemn the young men outright, or to emphasize a thematic link between the two schemes and argue that Farquhar is presenting serious social criticism here is a mistake. Comic values prevail: the thieves are foiled by the wittier young men; in a *deus ex machina* comic device, the elder brother dies and makes Aimwell no longer a counterfeit or in need of money; and before that, in an element of comic resolution new in English comedy, he abandons his pretence and confesses, reforming 'through sensibility and compassion'.[31] The beaux's stratagem is quarantined from criticism.

But if the play offers no opportunity for easy condemnation of the fortune-hunters' scheme, it does criticize the values of their world. A passage of conversation between the young men in I.i comments on the

30 *The Comedy of Manners* (London 1970), p. 153, reprinted in Anselment, ed., *The Recruiting Officer and The Beaux' Stratagem: a Casebook*, p. 157. Valentine is the hero of *Love for Love*, and Mirabell of *The Way of the World*.
31 John Traugott, 'The Rake's Progress from Court to Comedy', *Studies in English Literature*, 6 (1966), qtd. in Hume, *The Rakish Stage*, p. 172.

hypocrisy of a society which, whatever it pretends to value, in truth values only riches. The irony is scathing: 'there is no scandal like rags, nor any crime so shameful as poverty'. A well-dressed sharping rogue is welcome in Lord Aimwell's box at the theatre; a wealthy pickpocket marries 'a great fortune', while the young man of talent, good looks and intelligence is no one if he has no money. The figure of 'poor Jack Generous in the park' lingers in the memory: 'and though the Mall was crowded with company, yet was poor Jack as single and solitary as a lion in a desert'. Aimwell adds: 'And as much avoided, for no crime upon earth but the want of money' (I.i.137–8).

Restoration comedy is often satirical, at the expense of marriage, lawyers, fops, and amorous old ladies, but this awareness of poverty, and its humiliations, is unusual. It appears elsewhere in Farquhar's work. In *Love and a Bottle* the young Irishman Roebuck arrives in London with 'not one farthing in his pocket', and meets Cripple a beggar, 'a poor old soldier', who explains to him who is most likely to be charitable: certainly not a rich man, a clergyman or a beau. His speeches are amusing but cut deep (I.i.25–47). Farquhar, one cannot but think, because of his own experience, writes with an understanding of what life is without money. In *The Beaux' Stratagem*, for all the beaux' optimism and resourcefulness, there is an underlying sense of what miseries lie ahead if they fail to repair their fortunes. And if turning soldier becomes their only option, they may perish.

Later when their stratagem seems to be working, Aimwell has scruples: ''Sdeath, 'tis pity to deceive her' (IV.ii.3–4). Archer reminds him of their life in town without money, and they go over it in detail. Anything is better, Aimwell agrees, than the fact that they have outlived their fortunes becoming known among their acquaintance. When in Act V Aimwell reveals to Archer that he has confessed all to Dorinda the humiliation they were so desperate to avoid seems inevitable. Archer, furious, refuses to stay any longer: 'Stay! What, to be despised, exposed and laughed at? – No, I would sooner change conditions with the worst of the rogues we just now bound than bear one scornful smile from the proud knight [Sir Charles] that once I treated as my equal' (V.iv.56–9). To be seen to be unable to support one's position in society is unbearable.

This is a comedy which deals squarely with money and the 'want of money', meaning the lack of rather than the desire for it, from well before the moment when Mrs Sullen wittily attributes the preference of philosophers and poets for the country to their not having enough money for town. Open talk of the financial aspects of marriage was then, of course, not unusual. Mrs Sullen and Dorinda both have dowries of ten thousand pounds. Dorinda is delighted to think that she is making such an advantageous match in marrying Aimwell: 'there will be title, place, and precedence, the park, the play, and the drawing-room, splendour, equipage, noise and flambeaux' (IV.i.402–4). But when he confesses he is not Lord Aimwell, she proves her heroine status, valuing his virtue above wealth, and is pleased to think this demonstrates she was (unlike her brother) marrying for love alone. But then she has all along her ten thousand pound fortune.

A more unusual figure seeking to rise by marriage is Cherry. She has aspirations beyond her class, and believes herself not her father's child. Convinced that she is out of place in the Inn, she has provided money for herself to go up in the social world, but the secondary position of women in her society means she cannot do this alone. When the dashing young man flirts with her, teaching her 'Love's Catechism', she sees an attractive solution. Believing he is more than a footman, she offers Archer herself in marriage, and two thousand pounds. He instinctively turns her down. Though he would be quite happy, as he tells her, to go to bed with her, without the money, the idea of marrying 'an innkeeper's daughter' touches his pride. He may not have money to maintain his position, but, as demonstrated again later in his reaction to the arrival of Sir Charles, his pride is intact. The audience is presumably expected to approve the sentiments about the moral force of pride in one's rank which he expresses, in verse, marking the end of Act II. Cherry, loyal to the last, warns Aimwell about the burglary at Lady Bountiful's, sends Archer the strong box with two hundred pounds, and in a note promises him friendship to death. Archer is still not interested, and repays the absent Cherry only by asking that Dorinda take her as her maid in place of Gipsy. The role of the innkeeper's daughter proved a favourite in the eighteenth- and nineteenth-century perhaps not only because of her quick tongue and frankness, but also because her unusual ambitions made her such sympathetic figure. Audiences today too will share the director William Gaskill's wish that Farquhar had made more of this young woman's part.[32] She is off stage in Act V and this lessens the impact of Archer's final neglect of her. As another director of Farquhar rightly remarks: we must expect the leading figures of Restoration comedy to treat their inferiors with carelessness.[33]

---

32 Interview with William Gaskill [by Simon Trussler]: 'Finding a Style for Farquhar', *Theatre Quarterly*, I, i (1971), 15–20, 19.
33 Max Stafford-Clark, *Letters to George* (London 1990), p. 44; see also Interview with Gaskill, p. 18.

MARRIAGE, DIVORCE AND FEMINISM

The courtship done, the obstacles overcome, marriage is the conventional end of comedy. This is the case even in Restoration plays where, as Lady Woodvil has it, 'lewdness is the business now, love was the business in my time'.[34] In *The Country Wife* for instance, Harcourt and Alithea marry, although the rake Horner goes unpunished, and jealous Mr Pinchwife seems doomed to be cuckolded by his young wife, if he hasn't been already. But if, as Hume argues, marriage in almost all plays from 1660 to the death of Farquhar is desirable and indeed the norm, much attention goes to making comedy out of the unhappily married. Then, late in this period, plots began to emerge which move to the repair of marriage and the reform of rakish husbands. Cibber's *Love's Last Shift* (1696) does just that, with Vanbrugh being provoked to write *The Relapse* in reply.

While marriage is upheld, at the same time these later comedies also register a contemporary awareness that it may not be good for women. The challenge to the absolute power of the King which had seen the execution of one king, the deposition of another, and rule by a commonwealth, also provoked questioning of patriarchal authority, and saw the early stirrings of feminist writing on women's rights. In a time of arranged marriages among the well-to-do, some fathers and husbands became tyrants, abusing the power they had and treating women as slaves. Sarah Egerton was one of those women who wrote in protest against those claiming their power was sanctioned by the law and church: 'The husband with insulting tyranny / Can have ill manners justified by law, / For men all join to keep the wife in awe'.[35] Mary Astell, who chose to remain unmarried, wrote several prose tracts advising women to avoid marriage if possible since the risks of finding an unkind husband were so great. Mary, Lady Chudleigh's 'The Ladies' Defence', written in response to a sermon advocating total submission of wives to their husbands entitled 'The Bride Woman's Counsellor', acknowledged that if a 'generous few' wished women to be free from 'barbarous usage', most men were content to think of women as no more that toys or 'Puppets, to divert Mankind'.[36]

Farquhar creates the Sullens in the context of what was indeed a

---

34 William Wycherley, *The Man of Mode*, IV.i.
35 'The Emulation' (1703), *Eighteenth-Century Women Poets*, ed. Roger Lonsdale (Oxford 1989), p. 31.
36 'The Ladies Defence' (ll. 538, 548), *The Poems and Prose of Mary, Lady Chudleigh*, ed. Margaret J. M. Ezell (Oxford 1993), p. 31.

Dorinda (Sheila Reid) tries to cheer her sister-in-law, Mrs Sullen (II.i).

Archer (Robert Stephens) and Scrub (Bernard Gallagher) become 'sworn brothers' (III.iii).
Both pictures from National Theatre production, 1970, © Douglas Jeffery.

'sudden arousal of interest in the position of women in society'.[37] Mrs Sullen has apparently been married carelessly to Sullen, a substantial landowner pleased to find a wife with ten thousand pounds. The result is their mutual unhappiness. He is no tyrant, but they are totally incompatible. Though clearly related to Vanbrugh's Sir John Brute, Sullen is a more miserable, more convincing sot because less flamboyant. He drinks, Farquhar doesn't explain why: do the expectations his London wife has of him drive him to it? Loftis sees him as 'a memorable example of the brutish degeneration to which a retired country life can lead'.[38] To William Gaskill he was immediately recognizable: the man who 'really prefers drinking with people of a different social class'.[39]

The characterization of his wife, Mrs Sullen, is one of the great achievements of the play. The pathos of her situation, apparent from the first, is all the more telling because she is an affectionate, witty woman, making her life more bearable with mocking accounts of her husband. She takes steps to improve her situation, planning to arouse her husband's interest, and complaining to her brother. Unlike Lady Lurewell, the female rake in *The Constant Couple*, who wreaks vengeance on one man by taking many lovers, Mrs Sullen is life-like. Her involvement with the Count is chaste, but, in her lonely state, she melts before the greater attraction of Archer. Their scenes together are a prolonged sophisticated flirtation, played out in sexual innuendoes and double entendres, dialogue which in the hands of a pair of good actors, is theatrically electric. The question is always will she or won't she.

In the bedroom scene in Act V.ii she is clinging to virtue, resisting but almost giving in to Archer, when Scrub rushes in. But what she needs most is not a lover, but a divorce. She knows that obtaining one is most unlikely, and cries out against a law unqualified to 'prove the unaccountable disaffections of wedlock' (III.iii.396–7). In Farquhar's day couples might separate, but divorce, allowing remarriage, had to be obtained by Act of Parliament, and was extremely rare. Only six divorces were granted in the years between 1660 and 1714.[40] Mrs Sullen's complaints of being locked into marriage with a totally incompatible husband follow, often word for word, phrases in Milton's divorce pamphlets,

---

37 David Roberts, *The Ladies: Female patronage of Restoration Drama 1660–1700* (Oxford 1989), p. 144.
38 Loftis, *Comedy and Society*, p. 73.
39 Interview with Gaskill, p. 18. For more on the playing of Sullen, see pp. xxxiv and xxxvi–vii.
40 See Hume, *The Rakish Stage*, p. 180.

principally *The Doctrine and Discipline of Divorce*, but also *Tetrachordon*.[41] Farquhar must have had them open on his desk as he wrote. In his arguments to persuade the Parliament of England to change the law of divorce, Milton insists on the notion of marriage being created by God as a union of body and mind, of compatible people who can support each other. If a couple cannot achieve this, Milton argues that it is not God's intention, nor the law of Moses that they should be forced to remain together, unhappy, and lead each other into temptation; rather, it should be possible for them to divorce by mutual consent. Farquhar adapts Milton's passionate rhetoric for Mrs Sullen's exclamations to Dorinda and, because she is such a vital and witty woman, the phrases do not appear incongruous.

The end of the play comprises one marriage and, apparently, one divorce. But however dramatically appropriate the liberation of Mrs Sullen may be, it is legally impossible. Comedies, of course, often come to resolutions where what happens is desirable, though unreal, or most unlikely, as in Olivia's shifting her affection from Cesario to Sebastian in *Twelfth Night*, or the conversion of wicked Duke Frederick in *As You Like It*. There is no doubt that this divorce *ought* to be possible: but here the audience was asked to accept not a change of heart in one of the characters, but a change to the law of the land in which they lived. The resolution is a fantasy, as least for Farquhar's own audience. Whether Mrs Sullen and Archer, partners in the final dance, make a lasting relationship, the goal to which the affective movement of the play is driving, is, historically, a pointless question since Mrs Sullen is not 'free'. But for an audience seeing the play today a romantic solution is more readily available.

However romantic the ending in performance, the play dramatizes the ills of marriage, and the need for divorce reform, and gives a vivid sense of Mrs Sullen's pathetic situation which, as Muir remarks, could have been treated tragically.[42] Farquhar's interest in this question has been associated with his own financially unfortunate marriage which, some biographers assume, must also have been unhappy. But the evidence is simply not there to support this connection. Rather, Farquhar should be credited with sensitivity to a contemporary social problem, and with an incisive dramatization of an incompatible couple which manages to

41 Martin A. Larson pointed out these borrowings in 'The Influence of Milton's Divorce Tracts on Farquhar's *Beaux' Stratagem*', *PMLA*, 39 (1924), pp. 174–8.
42 Muir, *Comedy of Manners*, p. 150, reprinted in Anselment, ed., *The Recruiting Officer and The Beaux' Stratagem: a Casebook*, p. 154.

maintain a comic mood. It is of course possible to play this comedy more or less lightly, as a happy-ending romp or as an anti-romantic satire which asks how successful will be the marriage of Aimwell and Dorinda, and where Archer's appetite will lead him next.[43] But audiences then and now have a taste for romantic endings.

THE PLAY AND ITS CRITICS

Though Farquhar's last two plays have always been popular with audiences, with *The Beaux' Stratagem* generally thought the better of the two, the critical reception of his work has been less unanimous. The triumph of *The Constant Couple: or A Trip to the Jubilee* aroused such critical spite that one contemporary insisted its success lay solely in the novelty of its title. Farquhar was also vilified as a plagiarist, when he was in fact recycling his own work,[44] and *The Inconstant*, his adaptation of Fletcher, was damned for not equalling the original. The scorn he expressed in his 'Discourse on Comedy' for writers who revered Aristotle, not a poet, and wrote according to 'critical formalities' rather than to please and instruct a diverse audience with coherent characters, recognizable absurdities and the 'natural air of free conversation' not surprisingly also offended the critics. Pope's dismissive reference to his 'low pert dialogue',[45] given Pope's critical sway, clouded his reputation in the eighteenth century. The wholesale attack on the immorality of Restoration comedy, begun by Collier and others in Farquhar's life time, and given new force for Victorian readers by Macaulay in a review of Leigh Hunt's edition of plays by Wycherley, Congreve, Vanbrugh and Farquhar (1840), ensured that moral disapproval was likely to be an immediate reaction to his name. However, Hazlitt and others insisted on distinguishing Farquhar's comedies from the rest: Aimwell and Archer were 'real gentlemen and only pretended imposters', his heroes 'honest fellows at bottom'.[46] Farquhar's warm-hearted humanity and natural

---

43 Milhous and Hume, ch. 10, proposes and explores these alternatives.
44 Farquhar's short novel *The Adventures of Covent Garden* (1698) provided plot material and poems for *The Constant Couple*. *Love's Catechism* (1707), his contribution to a current vogue for catechisms, including *The Ladies Catechism* (1703) and *The Town Misses* [= whores'] *Catechism* (1703) reappears slightly reworked in II.i. For Farquhar's early critics, see E. N. James, *George Farquhar: A Reference Guide* (The Hague 1972) and Shirley Strum Kenny, 'Theatrical Warfare, 1695–1710', *Theatre Notebook*, 27 (1972–3), pp. 137–8.
45 'The First Epistle of the Second Book of Horace Imitated', l. 288. Cordner (pp. xviii–xix) mentions Horace Walpole's criticism of Farquhar as not 'genteel', not upper class, and argues that true gentility is Farquhar's concern.
46 William Hazlitt, 'Lectures on the English Comic Writers', *The Complete Works of William Hazlitt*, ed. P. P. Howe, 21 vols. (London 1930–1934), VI, 84–5.

characterization were again praised by Leigh Hunt and in 1904 by William Archer. Leigh Hunt claimed that of his four playwrights Farquhar possessed 'the truest dramatic genius, and the most likely to be of lasting popularity'. He is 'ten times acted to their one'.[47] Archer's enthusiasm is all the more striking since for him Wycherley and Vanbrugh meant 'absolute loathsomeness', and 'fetid brutality'. Farquhar rises above all this, his last two plays possessing 'a general tone of humanity', and 'a return to nature in the tone of the conversation'. *The Beaux' Stratagem* even meets Arnold's requirement that literature present 'a sober criticism of life'. This refers to the question of divorce. Farquhar had been accused of lacking of respect for the 'sanctity of the marriage tie' when the Sullens separate by mutual consent. On the contrary, Archer argues, Farquhar's plea for a more rational law of divorce is 'a homage to the idea of marriage which Wycherley, Congreve, or Vanbrugh would never have dreamt of paying'.[48]

Twentieth-century critics, with some exceptions less morally censorious, have complained that Farquhar is awkwardly transitional, combining the sharp brilliance of Restoration wit (though, according to some, not up to the level of Congreve) with sentimental episodes of the deplorable kind introduced into English comedy by Cibber and Steele. If Farquhar is, for his biographer Connely, the Restoration drama at twilight,[49] for others his sentimentality put the light out.[50] A more nuanced reading of Restoration comedy in the last half of the twentieth century, based on greater familiarity with the whole repertoire of plays, has broken down the monolith 'Restoration comedy' and led to a more accurate account of the variety of his work, his transitional position, and distinctive qualities in relation to Cibber, Steele and other post Restoration dramatists. Farquhar's interest in divorce, and sympathy with early feminist views has attracted critical attention. In this area, as in its criticism of attitudes to money, his play, though surprisingly 'modern', is questioning rather than subversive. He produces memorable scenes which expose what kind of people end up being asked to do the fighting in our wars, or what kind of miseries people suffer in marriage,

47 Leigh Hunt, *op. cit.*, p. lxii.
48 *George Farquhar*, ed. William Archer, Mermaid Series, (London 1906), p. 28.
49 William Connely's biography is *Young George Farquhar: The Restoration Drama at Twilight* (London 1949).
50 'Farquhar killed the comedy to which he contributed the last brilliant examples.' (John Palmer, *The Comedy of Manners* (1913), p. 242, rptd. in Anselment, *op. cit*, p. 53. Hazlitt was more generous: 'we may date the decline of English comedy from the time of Farquhar', *ed. cit.*, VI, 88.

and continually delights with his hallmark 'sprightly dialogue . . . expressive of fun, vivacity, and freshness of phrase, and with an ear close to the life round him'.[51]

Staging the Play at the Queen's Theatre

The new theatre in the Haymarket designed by Vanbrugh for opera and plays had been open for two years when *The Beaux' Stratagem* was first performed on 8 March 1707. It was on the edge of London. Fashionable squares and streets were soon to be built there, but at the time the surroundings were 'but so many green fields of pasture'.[52] Colley Cibber writes about the theatre at length in his autobiography because this 'vast, triumphal piece of architecture' had such bad acoustics, thanks to its great width and a very high ceiling over the auditorium and orchestra, that 'scarce one word in ten, could be distinctly heard in it'.[53] All the same, Farquhar's play enjoyed a huge success, though Cibber includes it among Queen's theatre plays which met 'much better reception' when transferred to Drury Lane. In theatres at this time, at the Queen's, as at Drury Lane and elsewhere, the action took place on the forestage, in front of the proscenium, with actors making entrances on and off through doors in the wall on either side of the stage, next to the first boxes. The socially diverse audience sat on three levels, the pit and two galleries, with boxes at the two lower levels. Farquhar viewed with mock horror the task of pleasing them all: 'here is a pit full of Covent-Garden gentlemen, a gallery full of cits, an hundred ladies of court education, and about two hundred footmen of nice morality'.[54]

Performances were lit by candles hung in great hoops over the stage, and supplemented by footlights. The auditorium was likewise lit by chandeliers. A green curtain was raised behind the proscenium to announce the beginning of the play and lowered only at the end of the performance, not between acts. The scenery consisted of pairs of flats or shutters, painted to resemble indoor or outdoor scenes, sometimes complete with furniture. High narrow pieces of scenery, or wings, made a border for the shutters. Pairs of shutters, chosen from the theatre's stock, set up behind each other, would provide a suitable background for the Inn, a room in Lady Bountiful's house, the gallery, and a bedroom. At the

51 Connely, p. 77.
52 Colley Cibber, *An Apology for the Life of Colley Cibber*, ed. B. R. S. Fone (Ann Arbor 1968), p. 173.
53 Cibber, *Apology*, p. 173; for plays transferred to Drury Lane, see p. 182.
54 'A Discourse upon Comedy', Kenny, II, 367.

end of a scene a pair were drawn open to reveal a new setting, or pushed closed to make another, and this was done in full view of the audience. Furniture and props were simple, a few glasses for Bonniface's inn, a chair for Aimwell, the largest piece here being the bed in V.ii, though a bed might have been painted on to one of the wings. At this time, actors did not usually venture into the up-stage area, among the scenery, but remained in the better lit forestage. Exceptions in this play are Gipsy's hiding to overhear: '*Goes behind the side-scene, and listens*' (IV.i.216), and, if the bed were painted on the scenery, Archer and Scrub's hiding behind it in V.ii. The change to another apartment in the same house for V.iii allows a bed to be removed. Actors in comedies dressed in the fashionable style of the day or in clothes appropriate to their character's occupation. Archer wears a footman's livery, though a rather dashing version of it, judging from Scrub's description (III.i.64–8). Actresses, as in V.ii, were shown off 'undressed' to the audience in innumerable closet or bedroom scenes, and in breeches roles, disguised as men. Music played an important part in both comedies and tragedies. A small orchestra played the 'first music' and then the 'second music' before the play began. The introduction of songs and a final dance were established features. Though Farquhar has been accused of failing to bring this play to a conclusion and lamely ending with a dance, an on-stage dance was a conventional ending of a comedy. The leading actors, men and women, were expected to sing, as Archer does here. Playwrights knew they had to compete with the rising popularity of opera. A frontispiece from 1737 of a performance at the Little Theatre in the Haymarket is the best illustration which has survived of these playing conditions. (See page xxx) Taken together, they made for what might strike us as a disjunctive experience, with minimal rather than naturalistic settings on one hand, and, on the other, close contact between the audience and the actors or the characters they played. The proximity, especially obvious in the small theatre, facilitated the playing of asides: pieces of dialogue such as Aimwell questioning Gibbet, where their asides convey a private sense of the interview (III.ii), presented no problems. These two, along with Dorinda, Aimwell, Archer, and Cherry take the audience into their confidence, and give the play 'a particularly open quality'.[55]

The audience was close to the actors also in the sense of being familiar with them. Regular theatre-goers would have been seeing the principal actors for several years, and known the kinds of roles they played.

---

55 Max Stafford-Clark, *Letters to George*, p. 151.

The Little Theatre in the Haymarket, 1737. © V & A Images/Victoria and Albert Museum

Farquhar knew the actors he was writing for; they were old acquaintances, though this was the first time his leading lady was Anne Oldfield, the brilliant actress whom, the story has it, he 'discovered' in her aunt's pub reading aloud a Fletcher play. Cibber praises her genius and 'the variety of her powers'. She had already been playing opposite the Irish actor Robert Wilks for some time. They were an established star couple, exactly what was needed for Mrs Sullen and Archer, to heighten expectations of their potentially romantic situation.[56] Wilks, who acted with Farquhar in Dublin, was the original Sir Harry Wildair in *The Constant Couple*. Mills who played Aimwell, was, as usual, playing the less flamboyant friend of the Wilks' character. Norris, who played Scrub, was another actor who leapt to fame in *The Constant Couple*, where he played Dicky the servant, and was forever after known as 'Jubilee Dicky'. Scrub, in the sense short tree or bush, is an allusion to his short stature. An actor of comic genius, he established the role that later attracted the finest actors, including Garrick.[57] Colley Cibber, famous as Lord Foppington in *The Relapse*, turned down the part of the servant Scrub and played Gibbet instead, a gentleman if only of the road.[58] Bonniface was played by the large actor, Bullock, who had previously played the drag role, Midnight the midwife in Farquhar's *The Twin-Rivals*, and the appealing country lad in *The Recruiting Officer* whom Farquhar had simply named Bullock. Casting continued to run true to type in the lesser roles: Mrs Powell (Lady Bountiful) played comic old women; Boman, who specialized in fops, the Frenchman Bellair; and Bowen, another Irishman, played Foigard. The most intriguing piece of casting was John Verbruggen as Sullen. Aged about forty, he had played Iago, Hotspur, and Alexander in *The Rival Queens*, as well as comic roles. Was he, as in the dramatis personae, 'the country blockhead', or was he a more threatening drunk? Milhous and Hume point out that when Verbruggen left the company

---

56 'Mrs Oldfield and Mr Wilks, by their frequently playing against one another, in our best comedies, very happily supported that humour and vivacity which is so peculiar to our English stage' (Cibber, *Apology*, p. 169).

57 See *Restoration and Georgian England; Theatre in Europe*, David Thomas and Arnold Hare, eds. (Cambridge 1989), pp. 378–9, for Lichtenberg's 1775 account of Garrick as Archer and Thomas Weston as Scrub, with Weston imitating the pose and gestures of Garrick's Archer, business that was played into the nineteenth century (see Barry N. Olshen, '*The Beaux' Stratagem* on the Nineteenth-Century London Stage', *Theatre Notebook*, 28 (1974), 70–80, 72–3).

58 Connely, pp. 295–6. Hazlitt reports that Weston was also a reluctant Scrub: 'It was much against his will that he was accidentally forced to play Scrub . . . when he threw everyone into raptures, except himself. Even the very boys followed him in the streets, exclaiming, "There – that's he that played Scrub." Hazlitt, *ed. cit.*, III, 77.

the role was taken over by the actor who had been playing Sir Charles, which rather suggests the latter.[59]

It is obvious that Farquhar, an actor himself, wrote for actors experienced in delivering elaborate comic language. He trusted them to handle quick dialogue, as in the catechism passage, and the more subtle playing of hints and innuendoes, Mrs Sullen and Archer especially, though Dorinda and Aimwell too are required to point double meanings in the scene of Aimwell's 'swoon', where everyone except Lady Bountiful understands what is happening. He also expected them to manage to extract various comic effects from the flowery rhetoric of love. When Aimwell is struck by Dorinda, 'she looked like Ceres in her harvest' (III.ii.7), Archer ridicules his romantic susceptibility and the audience is presumably invited to join him. When in IV.i Aimwell comes out of his 'swoon' and addresses Dorinda as a goddess, he is, though attracted to Dorinda, putting on an act, and Dorinda soon grasps what it is, and enjoys it. Archer then takes up the lover's exaggerated rhetoric and complimentary classical allusions to seduce Mrs Sullen: she too knows she is being flattered and also enjoys it. It is clear too what Archer wants, his high flown style a burlesque of high romance courtship, manipulated to get the lady: 'Lilies unfold their white, their fragrant charms, / When the warm sun thus darts into their arms. *Runs to her*' (V.ii.40–1).[60]

Recent Productions

Performances of the play in extraordinary places and circumstances testify to the phenomenal popularity of *The Beaux Stratagem*. In 1770, the Leeward Island Company played it in the town of Christiansted in the Caribbean.[61] Mrs Abington, the first Lady Teazle in *The School for Scandal*, paid another extraordinary, though many thought ill-judged, tribute to Farquhar's comic characterization when she chose to play Scrub, not only a male role but a servant, at a benefit night in 1786. In the twentieth century there were memorable revivals, notably in 1927 with Edith Evans as Mrs Sullen, then famous for her brilliant Millamant a few years earlier. More followed as nineteenth-century prejudice against

59 Milhous and Hume, pp. 298–9.
60 For a detailed examination of this scene, see J. L. Styan, *Restoration Comedy in Performance* (Cambridge, 1986), pp. 168–70.
61 Odai Johnson, 'The Leeward Islands Company', *Theatre Survey*, 44, 1 (2003), 29–42, 34. Another theatrical tribute is the title of Hannah Cowley's play, *The Belle's Stratagem* (1780), one of the most staged main pieces between 1776 and 1800. (Hume, *Rakish Stage*, p. 238).

Restoration comedy faded,[62] though, as noted earlier, some critics have always been aware that Farquhar was not Wycherley or Congreve. In the provinces, the first production at the Birmingham Repertory theatre in 1957 saw the young Albert Finney as Archer and Nancie Jackson as Mrs Sullen. Lady Bountiful waving a five foot-long sword over her head to repel the burglars, Archer and Scrub hiding under the bed, but facing the audience, Sullen in nightgown and cap, were comic moments in a production the critic J. C. Trewin found, like Dorinda in Act V, 'mighty gay'. He awarded Finney praise on behalf of 'Farquhar's gallant ghost' for adding 'style to enthusiasm', and, though he recalled earlier Mrs Sullens, 'the coloratura of Edith Evans or the sugar-plum coo of Kay Hammond', he admired Jackson's delivery of Farquhar's long sentences: this actress 'knows the tunes'. Moreover, Mrs Sullen is, he reminded his readers, 'a very real person'. Though this was not, Trewin remarked with suppressed distaste, 'everyone's favourite period of English comedy', the freshness of Farquhar was 'a current of air in the disorderly room'.[63]

The most significant production in the second half of the century was without doubt William Gaskill's for the National Theatre in 1970, which opened in Los Angeles, and then played in London. Gaskill had in 1963 chosen to direct *The Recruiting Officer* in the opening season of the National Theatre, and on the basis of this and later work, he is credited with demolishing the affected style of playing Restoration comedy, 'affected' meaning a style which, for no good reason, was felt to suit the conscious wit and brilliance of the language, and which in practice meant, in Gaskill's words, 'high camp, lisps, huge wigs, canes and fans'.[64] Instead, as Benedict Nightingale wrote, for Gaskill, Restoration comedy 'involves real people facing actual problems in a recognizable world,' an approach that works 'best for Farquhar, the most human and humane of all the Restoration dramatists'.[65] To prepare his actors, Gaskill insisted they 'go for the meaning', and therefore do 'a lot of work on the phrasing', something actors were no longer taught, to avoid breaking long sentences into too many sections. Actors playing the Lichfield characters were not to think in terms of accents. Sullen is not 'the conventional clown' or 'rustic buffoon'. Farquhar, in his view, was a

---

62 For nineteenth-century productions, and the cuts made with 'inordinate fastidiousness', see Olshen, cited above, note 44.

63 *The Birmingham Post*, 11 June 1957.

64 William Gaskill, *A Sense of Direction* (London 1988), p. 56; or, as Peter Wood put it: 'the language of the fan, the red heel and the patch', see Heather Neill, 'The show must go on', *The Times*, 25 August 1989.

65 *New Statesman*, 17 April 1970.

grown-up person, not 'sniggery' like Wycherley or 'mean-spirited' like Congreve. The actors' job was to play the human characters he had created. Admittedly Gibbet was 'slightly fantasticated'; to some extent so was Foigard. The actor of each of these Pistol-like characters had 'to make it clear that this is the character as written, not self-indulgence'.[66] Gaskill cut the role of the Count, feeling that it would harm Mrs Sullen's relationship with Archer if, after she had met him, she continued her scheme to take the Count as a lover, or to appear to, to rouse Sullen's feeling for her.

A backcloth of the city of Lichfield, with simple pieces flown in for the various indoor locations, provided light elegant settings. Thus the production's triumph belonged largely to Farquhar, to his 'serious comedy about divorce', 'comedy of the highest order', and to the actors' 'bell-like' delivery of the text.[67] Maggie Smith as Mrs Sullen gave 'a truly awesome performance', almost overwhelming her critics with her ability to convey changing states of mind with a phrase, a look or 'tiny deft movements of the head'.[68] One found it inconsistent that she teased the country-woman, but most could see her relieving her misery in bitter jokes. Robert Stephens's Archer received less attention, reflecting perhaps the dominance of Mrs Sullen in the play, in spite of the length of his role. Stephens in Los Angeles appeared not 'the familiar gay blade' but 'a calmer, more complicated, more worried fellow'.[69] In London he had become 'bold, gay, wanton', 'putting on a superb exhibition of genteel accomplishments in his test scene with the girls' (III.iii) and later with Mrs Sullen, as he goes through the courtship ritual, 'coming up to the mark with faultlessly phrased gallantries delivered through clenched teeth'.[70] The interplay between the two (he was, readers were reminded, Maggie Smith's husband) was compelling.

The actors avoided caricatures, except for Foigard and Gibbet who were naturally so. Bernard Gallagher played Scrub as seen from Scrub's own point of view. Gaskill's sense of Sullen convinced everyone; since he appears 'a perfectly rational man' (Wardle) when released from his marriage, there is no need to play him as a booby before that. Wardle also

---

66 Comments by Gaskill in this paragraph are from Interview with Gaskill.
67 First and third quotations: Irving Wardle, *The Times*, 6 September 1989; *Los Angeles Herald-Examiner*, 22 January 1970.
68 *Los Angeles Herald-Examiner; New Statesman*. Gaskill wrote of her Lady Pliant in *The Double Dealer:* 'It was immediately clear that she was the natural heiress to Edith Evans as the mistress of Restoration comedy' (*Sense of Direction*, p. 57).
69 *Los Angeles Herald-Examiner*.
70 Hilary Spurling, *The Spectator*, 18 April 1970; *The Times*, 9 April 1970.

Maggie Smith as Mrs Sullen in William Gaskill's National Theatre production, 1970, 'a truly awesome performance'. © Douglas Jeffery

commented on the Shavian quality of Archer, Bluntschli-like in his anti-romantic feeling. The programme carried John Mortimer's opinion that in *The Beaux' Stratagem* 'the English theatre looked, for the first time, with a cool and modern eye on the subject of divorce'. Here the ending, so earnestly discussed by critics, passed without need for clarification. It was its plea for divorce which impressed, in spite of a reformed divorce law, along with the serio-comic power of Mrs Sullen's situation.

The next major production in the United Kingdom was Peter Wood's, again at the National Theatre, in 1989. It was, *The Times* revealed, Wood's favourite play. From the reviews it emerges that though Wood 'loved' it, he did not trust it as thoroughly as Gaskill had done. The sets were more elaborate, there was incidental music, and more business, to the annoyance of Michael Billington: 'a totally misplaced piece of comic knockabout when Archer routs the Burglars'.[71] It was moreover thematically heavy-handed: Wood's determination to mine 'the whole text with references to marital misery' left it lacking comic zest.[72] Brenda Blethyn played Mrs Sullen. Blethyn was moved by the everyday commonness of her situation, telling an interviewer 'it's not a Restoration romp, it's actually very pertinent. . . . She calls her husband a drunken sot. He's out drinking with his mates when all she wants is a cuddle, some conversation and a bit of flattery.'[73] This production allowed her her lover, the Count, a romantic figure in a dark hat carrying a red rose, and proclaiming his Frenchness with a magnificent moustache. The reviews were divided between those who saw 'a complete success . . . a nearly unalloyed delight', an 'unsentimental view of how married couples exasperate and disgust each other',[74] and those who saw a 'dull and plodding production', an unequal cast, 'dull sets', with Lady Bountiful 'a little too opulent for a small town like Lichfield'.[75] Brenda Blethyn received unanimous praise for her sexually frustrated Mrs Sullen, both funny and in touch with 'the deep vein of pathos that is always lurking underneath Farquhar's polished surface'.[76] Marc Sinden fared less well. Those anticipating a comic rustic found 'an undistinguished morose fool when, to get its usual quota of laughs, he ought to be a rampaging,

71 Michael Billington, *The Guardian*, 7 September 1989.
72 *The Times*, 6 September 1989.
73 *Evening Standard*, 10 October 1989.
74 *Daily Telegraph*, 10 September 1989; Rhoda Koenig, *Punch*, Christmas 1989.
75 Milton Shulman, *Evening Standard*, 15 November 1989; *City Limits*, 22 November 1989; *Sunday Times*, 10 September 1989.
76 Christopher Edwards, *Spectator*, 25 November 1989.

brutish, insensitive clown';[77] those looking for 'sheer befuddled nastiness' found only rustic 'pear-shaped vowels'.[78] John Peter asked for a Sullen 'a touch more brutish' but otherwise approved: this was a 'smug, peremptory young man', totally unfit for marriage but otherwise harmless.[79] The 'modern', or Shavian quality of the play, detected in the 1970 Archer's anti-romantic moments, was discovered in this production in the debate between Sir Charles and Sullen about marriage, and also emanating from Cherry. Jessica Turner was 'not only devastatingly fetching but also intellectually on top of her London lover'.[80] Her catechism dialogue with Archer developed 'a huge erotic charge'.[81] Wood's admiration for Farquhar as a democratic writer, and one who knew how to make characters drive the plot, did not result in a production to banish memories of Gaskill's,[82] but it was enjoyed, and as Gaskill himself said, this is a play that it is easy to do reasonably well. Throughout the English speaking world it continues to attract performers, playing often as more of a romp than the productions discussed here. A graduate school performance at Yale in 1996 is an example: the Count 'makes his big opening with a flying leap on his way to seduce Mrs. Sullen ... he falls and screams loudly,' and a crocodile hanging from the inn ceiling growls when Gibbet thinks of hiding his loot in it. The review continues: 'Small gags of this nature fill the entire play in order to lighten this old classic and relate it to the modern day.'[83] The high spirits of the play may inspire such inventions, but as Gaskill and others have shown, they are not needed.

A Summary of the Plot

Aimwell and Archer, reduced to their last two hundred pounds, arrive at a Lichfield inn. They intend to restore their fortunes by marriage to a rich heiress, Aimwell presenting himself as Lord Aimwell, Archer as his 'footman' Martin. Bonniface, the innkeeper, who is in league with a gang of highwaymen, takes Aimwell for another. His daughter Cherry is attracted to the 'footman' Martin, and Archer to her.

---

77 *Evening Standard.*
78 *The Guardian;* it is fair to note that Sinden took over the role a week before the opening.
79 *Sunday Times,* 10 September 1989.
80 *The Guardian.*
81 *The Times.*
82 Max Stafford-Clark remarks that the success of Gaskill's 1963 *The Recruiting Officer,* and fear of comparison, had kept Farquhar's play off the stage for 30 years (*Letters to George,* p. 40).
83 Laaté Olukotun, *The Yale Herald,* 1 March 1996.

Archer (Stephen Dillon) and Aimwell disarm and bind the burglars Bagshot and Hounslow (David Annen and Anthony Renshaw) (V.iii) before delivering them to Scrub (Allan Corduner) in Peter Wood's National Theatre Production, 1989. © Clive Barda/ArenaPAL.

Act II scene i introduces Mrs Sullen and her sister-in-law, Dorinda. Neglected by her boorish husband, Mrs Sullen plans to arouse his interest by feigning a liaison with the French Count. Aimwell sets out for church to find a rich beauty. Cherry, convinced 'Martin' is more than a footman, offers him herself and her fortune in return for marriage. Archer refuses, unable to bring himself to marry an innkeeper's daughter.

Dorinda has noticed Aimwell at church and fallen in love with him. She sends the servant Scrub to invite the footman to share a bottle of ale so she and Mrs Sullen may question him about his master. Archer congratulates Aimwell on locating a fortune of ten thousand pounds and warns him against romantic feelings. He accepts Scrub's invitation, intrigued by hearing of Dorinda's 'very handsome' companion. Aimwell encounters Gibbet, a highwayman passing as a Captain, and the Irishman Foigard, passing as a French priest.

Scrub reveals to 'Martin' his love for the maid Gipsy and his fear that she favours Foigard. Mrs Sullen and Dorinda question 'Martin'. Mrs Sullen likes him and is convinced he is more than a footman. Mrs Sullen puts her plot into practice but Sullen is unmoved by his wife's having a suitor. She apologises to the Count for making use of him.

A country-woman arrives to seek help from Lady Bountiful. Mrs Sullen mocks her misfortunes because saddened by her own. Archer announces that his master has been taken ill in the garden. He is brought in seated in a chair. While Lady Bountiful ministers to him he holds Dorinda's hand, and murmurs her praises. At the same time, Mrs Sullen and Archer express interest in each other. Once Aimwell is recovered, the four go off to view Lady Bountiful's pictures.

Foigard bribes Gipsy on behalf of the disappointed Count. She agrees to hide the Count in a closet in Mrs Sullen's bedchamber. Archer continues to woo Mrs Sullen with witty flattery. Scrub overhears the Count's plot and tells his 'brother Martin' of it. The ladies compare their lovers' speeches: Mrs Sullen wonders if she can resist temptation.

In the Inn Archer and Aimwell threaten Foigard with death for being an English subject in the service of the French, and trick him into admitting he is Irish. In return for his life Foigard agrees to put Archer in the bedchamber instead of the Count. Gibbet and his gang set out to rob Lady Bountiful's house.

That same night Sir Charles Freeman arrives at the Inn and encounters Sullen, his brother-in-law. Sullen agrees to hand over his troublesome wife. Cherry rouses Aimwell with the news of the robbery and he sets out to save Dorinda. She and Mrs Sullen are about to go to bed. Left alone Mrs Sullen imagines the 'lovely fellow' kneeling at her feet; she turns and finds him there. Archer urges her to be his; she wavers between resistance and surrender. As he is carrying her off Scrub enters saying thieves have broken into the house. He and Archer hide under the bed. Gibbet comes in and Archer seizes him. Together, Aimwell and Archer tie up the burglars and they are marched off to the cellar. Archer insists Aimwell now secure the fortune: the priest is at hand. Aimwell slips away with Dorinda. Just then Sir Charles is announced. Archer knows him and fears their project is ruined.

Aimwell is moved to confess all to Dorinda. Her reaction is to admire his honesty, but she dismisses the priest and leaves. Archer comes to congratulate Aimwell and hears he has confessed. He is disgusted. Aimwell still has hopes. Dorinda announces the death of his brother: he *is* Lord Aimwell and may marry her openly. Under their agreement Archer claims half of the lady's fortune. Aimwell offers him the lady or the fortune. Archer takes the money. Cherry is rewarded by being appointed Dorinda's maid. Sullen is ready to hand over his wife to Sir Charles, and the couple agree to part. Sullen is forced to hand over her fortune as well, since Archer, as a result of the burglary, has all Sullen's documents. Sullen invites everyone to celebrate a divorce and a wedding in his house, and Archer leads Mrs Sullen in a final dance.

A Note on the Text

The copy-text is a copy of the first edition, the quarto printed by Bernard Lintott on 27 March 1707, held in the Bodleian Library, University of Oxford, shelf mark Mal. 138(7). Lintott had bought the rights two months earlier on 27 January for thirty pounds (twice as much as he had paid for Farquhar's previous play, *The Recruiting Officer*). It is a 'clear and readable' text, as Kenny says, with some minor errors being corrected in printing, as is clear from variants in different copies. For instance: at III.iii.378 this copy has *be* while Kenny notes that Q has *de*, corrected to *be* in *Comedies* [1708]. More errors were corrected in Q2, a version identical to Q but for three minor changes in pagination. This edition adopts the emendation proposed by Roper for the play's crux at I.i.159–62. One unusual feature of the Bodleian copy (and of one other surviving copy) is the folding of the first sheet inside out with the result that the order of appearance of title page, advertisement, prologue etc., is jumbled. The correct order has been restored here, with the details of the misfolding recorded in the notes. The full texts of the songs in Act I, 'But you look so bright', and Act III.iii, 'A trifling song you shall hear', are reprinted from the 1728 sixth edition of Farquhar's *Works*, where they appear for the first time. This edition, which incorporates theatrical revisions of other Farquhar plays, is the first to record that the Count was cut out of Act III.iii by the author after the first night (according to a footnote) and his lines in V.iv given to Foigard. This entailed replacing the Count's French-English with Foigard's Irish attempt at French-English. The lines on Mrs Sullen's portion (V.iv.246–8) were also rewritten, with Archer making a stronger plea for Mrs Sullen's hand than in the original. Farquhar may be the author of these revisions (printed in the Appendix, pp. 135–6) though both his state of health, and the lines' heavy-handed stage-Irish, make that unlikely.

The names of the characters have been expanded from the Quarto abbreviations. Spelling and punctuation have been modernized throughout. One idiosyncrasy of the original punctuation, the use of the dash, is retained in cases where, as Trussler argues in his edition, it marks a pause or beat in a speech. Thus this edition, Cordner, and Trussler all print: 'Though the whining part be out of doors in town, 'tis still in force with the country ladies. – And let me tell you, Frank, the fool in that passion shall outdo the knave at anytime' (I.ii.214–16), where Q has 'ladies; – And let me'. The abbreviations 'em and 'um have been regularized to 'em, and look'e, look'ee, look'ye, etc., to look ye. Stage directions reproduce the original text, with any supplied by the editor placed in square brackets.

FURTHER READING

Editions
Michael Cordner, ed., *The Beaux' Stratagem*, The New Mermaids (1976)

Charles N. Fifer, ed., *The Beaux' Stratagem*, Regents Restoration Drama Series (1978)

Shirley Strum Kenny, ed., *The Works of George Farquhar*, 2 vols. (Oxford 1988)

William Myers, ed., *The Recruiting Officer and other plays* (Oxford 1995)

Staging
Emmett L. Avery, ed., *The London Stage Part 2: 1700–1729* (Carbondale 1968)

Interview with William Gaskill [by Simon Trussler]: 'Finding a Style for Farquhar', *Theatre Quarterly*, I, i (1971), 15–20

Barry N. Olshen, 'The Beaux' Stratagem on the Nineteenth-Century London Stage', *Theatre Notebook*, 28 (1974), 70–80

Philip H. Highfill Jr. et al., *A Biographical Dictionary of Actors, Actresses, Musicians, Dancers, Managers and Other Stage Personnel in London, 1660–1800* (Carbondale 1973–93)

Robert D. Hume, ed., *The London Theatre World, 1660–1800* (Carbondale 1980)

Judith Milhous and Robert D. Hume, *Producible Interpretation: Eight English plays, 1675–1707* (Carbondale 1985)

J. L. Styan, *Restoration Comedy in Performance* (Cambridge 1986)

Max Stafford-Clark, *Letters to George* (London 1990)

Tiffany Stern, *Rehearsal from Shakespeare to Sheridan* (Oxford 2000)

Biographical and critical studies
Martin A. Larson, 'The Influence of Milton's Divorce Tracts on Farquhar's *Beaux' Stratagem*', *PMLA*, 39 (1924), 174–8

James R. Sutherland, 'New Light on George Farquhar', *TLS*, 6 March 1937, p. 171

William Connely, *Young George Farquhar: The Restoration Drama at Twilight* (London 1949)

John Loftis, *Comedy and Society from Congreve to Fielding* (Stanford 1959)

Eric Rothstein, *George Farquhar* (New York 1967)

Alan Roper, '*The Beaux' Stratagem*: Image and Action', in Earl Miner, ed., *Seventeenth-Century Imagery: Essays on Uses of Figurative Language from Donne to Farquhar* (Berkeley 1971), pp. 169–86

Robert J. Jordan, 'George Farquhar's Military Career', *Huntington Library Quarterly*, 37 (1974), 251–64

Raymond A. Anselment, ed., *The Recruiting Officer and The Beaux' Stratagem: a Casebook* (Basingstoke 1977)

Shirley Strum Kenny, 'Humane Comedy', *Modern Philology*, 75 (1977), 29–43

Verlyn Flieger, 'Notes on the Titling of George Farquhar's *The Beaux' Stratagem*', *Notes and Queries*, 26 (1979), 21–23

Robert D. Hume, *The Rakish Stage: Studies in English Drama, 1660–1800* (Carbondale 1983)

E. N. James, *George Farquhar: a Reference Guide* (Boston 1986)

Richard W. Bevis, *English Drama: Restoration and the Eighteenth Century, 1660–1789* (London 1988)

David Roberts, *The Ladies: Female Patronage of Restoration Drama 1660–1700* (Oxford 1989)

Alan Roper, 'How much did Farquhar's Beaux Spend in London?', *Studies in Bibliography*, 45 (1992), 105–112

James E. Evans, 'Resisting a Private Tyranny in Two Humane Comedies' in Katherine M. Quinsey, ed., *Broken Boundaries: Women and Feminism in Restoration Drama* (Lexington 1996), pp. 150–63

John Bull, *Vanbrugh and Farquhar* (Houndmills 1998)

ABBREVIATIONS

1728	*The Works of the late Ingenious Mr George Farquhar*, sixth edn. (London 1728)
Comedies [1708]	*The Comedies of Mr George Farquhar* (London 1708), second edn. (1711)
Cordner	Michael Cordner, ed., *The Beaux' Stratagem*, The New Mermaids (1976)
Fifer	Charles N. Fifer, ed., *The Beaux' Stratagem*, Regents Restoration Drama Series (1978)
Jeffares	A. Norman Jeffares, ed., *The Beaux' Stratagem* (Edinburgh 1972)
Johnson's *Dictionary*	Samuel Johnson, *A Dictionary of the English Language,* (1755) (Hildesheim 1968)
Kenny	Shirley Strum Kenny, ed., *The Works of George Farquhar*, 2 vols. (Oxford 1988)
Milhous and Hume	Judith Milhous and Robert D. Hume, *Producible Interpretation: Eight English Plays, 1675–1707* (Carbondale 1985)
Myers	William Myers, ed., George Farquhar, *The Recruiting Officer and other plays* (Oxford 1995)
OED	*Oxford English Dictionary*
Prose Works	*Complete Prose Works of John Milton*, Gen. ed. Dom M. Wolfe 8 vols. (Newhaven 1953–1982) vol. II, 1959
Q	*The Beaux' Stratagem. A Comedy* (1707)
Q2	*The Beaux' Stratagem. A Comedy* (1707) (corrected)

TLS   *Times Literary Supplement*

Trussler   Simon Trussler, ed., *The Beaux' Stratagem* (1995)

KEY

A GUIDE TO THE EDITED VERSION OF THE PLAY TEXT

Copy-text = the earliest authorised version of the text. This is explained in the Note on the Text.
New Mermaids preserve the words of the original copy-text, and the verse lineation, but modernise spelling and punctuation, making the plays more accessible to readers.

s.p. = speech prefix, these are in CAPITALS

s.d. = stage direction. These are printed in italic to distinguish them from the spoken text. Additional stage directions inserted by the Editor for clarification are in [square brackets]. A stage direction that is centred denotes a key moment of action in the play.

Square brackets also mark significant editorial additions to the copy-text.

Verse lines are
                    Staggered when distributed between
                                        Two or more speakers

ed. = editorial emendation: wherever the editor has made a substantial change to the copy-text this is recorded in a footnote. The footnote will give the emended reading followed in brackets by the copy-text reading. The editor may also add a note in explanation.

Notes to the title page
The Title Page of the First Edition
reproduced with the permission of the Bodleian Library, University of Oxford

THE BEAUX STRATAGEM The title used for printed versions of the play; in play-bills and theatre records until the late eighteenth-century it was known as *The Stratagem.*

As it is Acted This phrase, usual at the time, indicates the near-simultaneous publication and performance of new plays. See Peter Holland, *The Ornament of Action: Text and performance in Restoration comedy* (Cambridge 1979), p. 106.

QUEEN'S THEATRE This grand new theatre, designed by Vanbrugh for drama and opera, opened in April 1705, and proved ill-suited for plays. See p. xxviii.

Author of the Recruiting-Officer Farquhar's most recent (1706) and highly successful comedy

LINTOTT also publisher of *The Recruiting Officer*, and the two previous Farquhar comedies

THE
Beaux Stratagem.
A
COMEDY.

As it is Acted at the

QUEEN's THEATRE

IN THE

HAY-MARKET.

BY

Her MAJESTY's Sworn Comedians.

Written by Mr. Farquhar, *Author of the* Recruiting-Officer.

LONDON:

Printed for BERNARD LINTOTT, at the *Cross-Keys* next
Nando's Coffee-House in *Fleetstreet.* 1707.

ADVERTISEMENT

The reader may find some faults in this play, which my illness prevented the amending of, but there is great amends made in the representation, which cannot be matched, no more than the friendly and indefatigable care of Mr Wilks, to whom I chiefly owe the success of the play.

GEORGE FARQUHAR

That Farquhar composed no dedication for his play, only this brief note, reflects his desperate situation.

PROLOGUE

When strife disturbs or sloth corrupts an age,
Keen satire is the business of the stage.
When the Plain-Dealer writ, he lashed those crimes
Which then infested most the modish times.
But now, when faction sleeps and sloth is fled,   5
And all our youth in active fields are bred;
When through Great Britain's fair extensive round,
The trumps of fame the notes of union sound;
When Anna's sceptre points the laws their course,
And her example gives her precepts force: 10
There scarce is room for satire; all our lays
Must be, or songs of triumph, or of praise.
But as in grounds best cultivated, tares
And poppies rise among the golden ears;
Our products so, fit for the field or school,   15
Must mix with nature's favourite plant – a fool:
A weed that has to twenty summers ran,
Shoots up in stalk, and vegetates to man.
Simpling our author goes from field to field,
And culls such fools, as may diversion yield;   20
And, thanks to nature, there's no want of those,

Written by Farquhar himself, as were the prologues to *Sir Harry Wildair*, *The Twin-Rivals* and *The Recruiting Officer*.

Mr Wilks player of Archer, and already mentioned gratefully in the Advertisement; for more on his connection with Farquhar see pp. vii–ix.

3 *the Plain-Dealer* William Wycherley (1640–1716), author of the much admired comedy of this name (1676), most recently revived in November 1705

4 *most the modish times* ed. (most – The Modish Times Q)

5–6 i.e. strife at home between Protestant and Catholic is over, and the country is busily engaged in the War of the Spanish Succession (1702–13).

8 Referring to the bill for the union of England and Scotland given royal assent on 6 March 1707, two days before the first performance of *The Beaux' Stratagem*.

19 *Anna* Anne, Queen of England, 1702–14, sister of William III and a devout Protestant

19 *Simpling* Collecting simples, i.e. medicinal herbs

20 *culls* selects, chooses

For rain, or shine, the thriving coxcomb grows.
Follies tonight we show, ne'er lashed before,
Yet, such as nature shows you every hour;
Nor can the pictures give a just offence,   25
For fools are made for jests to men of sense.

22 *coxcomb* a foolish person, from the cap in the shape of a cock's comb worn by the professional fool
23 *Follies . . . before* An overstatement: it is hard to identify follies in the play never before presented on the stage.
25 the satirist's traditional defence

DRAMATIS PERSONÆ

[AND ORIGINAL CAST]

MEN

AIMWELL ⎱	Two gentlemen of broken fortunes,	*Mr Mills*
ARCHER ⎰	the first as master, and the second as servant	*Mr Wilks*
COUNT BELLAIR	A French officer, prisoner at Lichfield	*Mr Bowman*
SULLEN	A country blockhead, brutal to his wife	*Mr Verbruggen*
FREEMAN	A gentleman from London	*Mr Keen*
FOIGARD	A priest, chaplain to the French officers	*Mr Bowen*
GIBBET	A highwayman	*Mr Cibber*
HOUNSLOW ⎱	His companions	
BAGSHOT ⎰		
BONNIFACE	Landlord of the inn	*Mr Bullock*
SCRUB	Servant to Mr Sullen	*Mr Norris*

4 *broken fortunes* When the play was first referred to in the press it was entitled *The Broken Beaux*.

7 *BELLAIR* handsome manner (French)

8 *Lichfield* the now accepted spelling (Litchfield Q, and throughout)

12 *FOIGARD* shield of faith (French)

15–16 *HOUNSLOW, BAGSHOT* places on major roads from London to the south and west, and the haunts of highwaymen

17 *BONNIFACE* from the Latin *bonum facere*, to do good; also of pretty appearance, 'bonny face', both here ironically applied

18 *SCRUB* a drudge, a hard-worked servant

WOMEN

LADY BOUNTIFUL	An old civil country gentlewoman that cures all her neighbours of all distempers, and foolishly fond of her son, *Sullen*	*Mrs Powell*
DORINDA	Lady Bountiful's daughter	*Mrs Bradshaw*
MRS SULLEN	Her daughter-in-law	*Mrs Oldfield*
GIPSY	Maid to the ladies	*Mrs Mills*
CHERRY	The landlord's daughter in the inn	*Mrs Bicknell*

[TAPSTER, SERVANT, FELLOW, COUNTRYWOMAN]

SCENE: *Lichfield*

2 *LADY BOUNTIFUL* The name is Farquhar's invention; 'since used for the great (or benefi-cent) lady in a neighbourhood' (*OED*).

ACT I. SCENE i

Scene, an inn

Enter BONNIFACE *running*

BONNIFACE
Chamberlain! Maid! Cherry! Daughter Cherry! All asleep, all
dead?

Enter CHERRY *running*

CHERRY
Here, here! Why d'ye bawl so, father? D'ye think we have no ears?
BONNIFACE
You deserve to have none, you young minx! – The company
of the Warrington coach has stood in the hall this hour, and   5
nobody to show them to their chambers.
CHERRY
And let 'em wait further; there's neither red-coat in the coach,
nor footman behind it.
BONNIFACE
But they threaten to go to another inn tonight.
CHERRY
That they dare not, for fear the coachman should overturn them   10
tomorrow. – Coming, coming! Here's the London coach arrived.

*Enter several people with trunks, bandboxes, and other luggage,
and cross the stage*

BONNIFACE
Welcome, ladies.

---

1 *Chamberlain* servant in charge of bedrooms
4 *deserve to have none* ears were cut off as a form of judicial punishment
5 *Warrington* town in Cheshire north-east of Lichfield on the Liverpool road
7–8 *neither red-coat . . . nor footman* neither a soldier nor someone travelling with servants;
footman 'a man-servant in livery employed chiefly to attend the carriage and wait at
table' *OED*, citing this passage as the first record of this meaning
11 s.d. *bandboxes* originally, as here, boxes for carrying bands (collars) and ruffs

CHERRY

Very welcome, gentlemen. – Chamberlain, show the Lion and
the Rose.

Exit with the company

Enter AIMWELL *in riding habit,* ARCHER *as footman
carrying a portmantle*

BONNIFACE

This way, this way, gentlemen.   15

AIMWELL

Set down the things; go to the stable, and see my horses well
rubbed.

ARCHER

I shall, sir.   *Exit*

AIMWELL

You're my landlord, I suppose?

BONNIFACE

Yes, sir, I'm old Will Bonniface, pretty well known upon this   20
road, as the saying is.

AIMWELL

O Mr Bonniface, your servant.

BONNIFACE

O sir. – What will your honour please to drink, as the saying is?

AIMWELL

I have heard your town of Lichfield much famed for ale. I think
I'll taste that.   25

BONNIFACE

Sir, I have now in my cellar ten tun of the best ale in
Staffordshire; 'tis smooth as oil, sweet as milk, clear as amber,
and strong as brandy; and will be just fourteen year old the fifth
day of next March, old style.

AIMWELL

You're very exact, I find, in the age of your ale.   30

---

13 *the Lion and the Rose* inn rooms referred to by name
14 s.d. *portmantle* a portmanteau, a case for carrying clothing
26 *tun* a large cask or barrel
29 *old style* i.e. according to the Julian calendar with, in England, the legal year beginning on
March 25. Though the New Style Gregorian calendar had been formally adopted in 1582
no adjustment was made until 1752, by which time England was 11 days behind the rest
of Europe.

BONNIFACE

As punctual, sir, as I am in the age of my children. I'll show you
such ale! – Here, tapster, broach number 1706, as the saying is
– Sir, you shall taste my *Anno Domini.* – I have lived in Lichfield
man and boy above eight and fifty years, and I believe have not
consumed eight and fifty ounces of meat.   35

AIMWELL

At a meal, you mean, if one may guess your sense by your
bulk.

BONNIFACE

Not in my life, sir; I have fed purely upon ale. I have eat my ale,
drank my ale, and I always sleep upon ale.

Enter tapster with a bottle and glass

Now, sir, you shall see. – (*Filling it out*) Your worship's health.   40
Ha! Delicious, delicious, – fancy it burgundy, only fancy it, and
'tis worth ten shillings a quart.

AIMWELL

(*Drinks*) 'Tis confounded strong.

BONNIFACE

Strong! It must be so, or how should we be strong that drink it?

AIMWELL

And have you lived so long upon this ale, landlord?   45

BONNIFACE

Eight and fifty years, upon my credit, sir; but it killed my wife,
poor woman, as the saying is.

AIMWELL

How came that to pass?

BONNIFACE

I don't know how, sir; she would not let the ale take its natural
course, sir, she was for qualifying it every now and then with a   50
dram, as the saying is; and an honest gentleman that came this
way from Ireland made her a present of a dozen bottles of

---

32 *number 1706* This sounds like last year's ale, not the fourteen year-old brew he promised.
36–7 *by your bulk* Compare *Mr Guts* (V.i.51).
39 s.d. *glass* glassware (Jeffares)
40 s.d. *Filling it out* Pouring it out (Fifer)

usquebaugh – but the poor woman was never well after. But,
however, I was obliged to the gentleman, you know.

AIMWELL

Why, was it the usquebaugh that killed her?   55

BONNIFACE

My Lady Bountiful said so. – She, good lady, did what could be
done; she cured her of three tympanies, but the fourth carried
her off. But she's happy, and I'm contented, as the saying is.

AIMWELL

Who's that Lady Bountiful you mentioned?

BONNIFACE

Ods my life, sir, we'll drink her health. (*Drinks*) My Lady   60
Bountiful is one of the best of women. Her last husband, Sir
Charles Bountiful, left her worth a thousand pound a year; and
I believe she lays out one half on't in charitable uses for the
good of her neighbours. She cures rheumatisms, ruptures, and
broken shins in men; green-sickness, obstructions, and fits   65
of the mother in women; the King's evil, chin-cough, and
chilblains in children; in short, she has cured more people in
and about Lichfield within ten years than the doctors have
killed in twenty; and that's a bold word.

AIMWELL

Has the lady been any other way useful in her generation?   70

---

53 *usquebaugh* whisky (Irish and Scottish Gaelic)

57 *tympanies* morbid swellings

65 *green-sickness* chlorosis, a form of anaemia seen in young women at puberty, attributed
in early modern medicine to virginity, but now associated with anorexia nervosa

65–6 *fits of the mother* hysteria, or a fit of suffocation in women and also men, so called
because in early medicine it was attributed to air rising from the womb or belly; compare
King Lear II.ii.246–7: 'O how this mother swells up toward my heart. / *Hysterica passio*,
down, thou climbing sorrow'.

66 *the King's evil* scrofula, a skin disease cured, some believed, by the King's touch; the
devout Queen Anne was the last monarch to perform this rite.
chin-cough whooping cough

68–9 Before medical advances in the nineteenth century Bonniface's poor opinion of doctors' cures in contrast to the remedies prepared by such 'female healers' as Lady Bountiful was a reasonable view to hold. See Roy Porter, *Disease, Medicine and Society in
England, 1550–1860*, 2nd ed. (Basingstoke 1993), ch. 2.

70 *Has . . . generation* Has she been useful also in producing children? Cordner compares the
remark of Sir Paul Pliant (married to a reluctant wife) in Congreve's *The Double-Dealer*,
III.i: 'alas, what's once a year to an old man who would do good in his generation?'

BONNIFACE

Yes, sir, she has a daughter by Sir Charles, the finest woman in all our country, and the greatest fortune. She has a son too by her first husband, Squire Sullen, who married a fine lady from London t'other day; if you please, sir, we'll drink his health.

AIMWELL

What sort of a man is he?   75

BONNIFACE

Why, sir, the man's well enough; says little, thinks less, and does – nothing at all, faith. But he's a man of great estate, and values nobody.

AIMWELL

A sportsman, I suppose?

BONNIFACE

Yes, sir, he's a man of pleasure; he plays at whisk, and smokes   80
his pipe eight and forty hours together sometimes.

AIMWELL

And married, you say?

BONNIFACE

Ay, and to a curious woman, sir. – But he's a – he wants it, here, sir. (*Pointing to his forehead*)

AIMWELL

He has it there, you mean?   85

BONNIFACE

That's none of my business, he's my landlord, and so a man you know, would not – But – ecod, he's no better than – Sir, my humble service to you. (*Drinks*) Though I value not a farthing what he can do to me; I pay him his rent at quarter-day, I have a good running trade, I have but one daughter, and I can give   90
her – but no matter for that.

AIMWELL

You're very happy, Mr Bonniface. Pray what other company have you in town?

---

80 *whisk* an earlier name of the card game whist
85 *He . . . mean* Bonniface implies that Sullen is 'a bit missing', or stupid, Aimwell that he has the horns of the cuckold: his wife is unfaithful.
87 *ecod* a mild oath, by God (also *egad*)
89 *quarter-day* traditional days for settling accounts (March 25, June 29, September 25, December 25)
90 *a good running trade* a regular income from the business; *running*: 'of trade, giving a certain turnover', *OED*, citing this line

BONNIFACE

A power of fine ladies, and then we have the French officers.

AIMWELL

O, that's right, you have a good many of those gentlemen. Pray   95
how do you like their company?

BONNIFACE

So well, as the saying is, that I could wish we had as many more
of 'em; they're full of money, and pay double for everything
they have. They know, sir, that we paid good round taxes for
the taking of 'em, and so they are willing to reimburse us a little.   100
One of 'em lodges in my house.

Enter ARCHER

ARCHER

Landlord, there are some French gentlemen below that ask for
you.

BONNIFACE

I'll wait on 'em. – (*To* ARCHER) Does your master stay long in
town, as the saying is?   105

ARCHER

I can't tell, as the saying is.

BONNIFACE

Come from London?

ARCHER

No.

BONNIFACE

Going to London, mayhap?

ARCHER

No.   110

BONNIFACE

[*Aside*] An odd fellow this. [*To* AIMWELL] I beg your worship's
pardon, I'll wait on you in half a minute.   *Exit*

---

94 *power of* large number of
   French officers Prisoners taken at the battle of Blenheim were released on parole in
   provincial towns. Justice Balance of Shrewsbury in *The Recruiting Officer* praises this
   victory to Captain Plume: 'but now ye have brought us colours and standards and
   prisoners' (*The Recruiting Officer*, ed. John Ross (2nd ed. 1991), II.i.6–7).
99 *paid . . . taxes* taxes levied to fund the war, notably a four shilling land tax

AIMWELL

The coast's clear, I see. – Now, my dear Archer, welcome to
Lichfield!

ARCHER

I thank thee, my dear brother in iniquity.   115

AIMWELL

Iniquity! Prithee leave canting, you need not change your style
with your dress.

ARCHER

Don't mistake me, Aimwell, for 'tis still my maxim that there
is no scandal like rags, nor any crime so shameful as poverty.

AIMWELL

The world confesses it everyday in its practice, though men   120
won't own it for their opinion. Who did that worthy lord,
my brother, single out of the side-box to sup with him t'other
night?

ARCHER

Jack Handycraft, a handsome, well-dressed, mannerly,
sharping rogue, who keeps the best company in town.   125

AIMWELL

Right! And, pray, who married my Lady Manslaughter t'other
day, the great fortune?

ARCHER

Why, Nick Marrabone, a professed pickpocket, and a good

---

116 *canting* using biblical language hypocritically, as in Archer's use of *iniquity*. Compare
  III.iii.389.

118–19 *my maxim . . . poverty* This is the first of several passages which also appear, some
  with slight variation, in Farquhar's *Love's Catechism* (see page xxvi, note 44 for the
  vogue in catechisms). The dialogue between Tom and Betty explains how poverty is a
  hindrance to love: Betty. *Because 'tis a Maxim now a-days, that there's no Scandal like
  Rags, nor any Crime so shameful as Poverty.* Tom. *How must a man remedy this?* Betty.
  *Why the World's wide enough, let Men bustle; for Fortune has taken Fools under her
  Protection, but Men of Sense are left to their Industry.'* (Kenny, II, 456) For the 'remedy',
  compare ll. 140–2 below.

122 *side-box* box at the side rather than rear of the theatre, where spectators were themselves
  on show, and so a favourite with the 'beaux'

125 *sharping* swindling, cheating

128 *Nick Marrabone* Like 'Handycraft' and 'Manslaughter', a significant name: 'to nick' is to
  steal, cheat; and 'nick' is a winning throw at dice; 'Marrabone' is a version of Maryle-
  bone, the London district noted at this time for bowling greens and gambling houses.
  Bowlers, once proverbially honest, were now developing a criminal reputation. Jeffares
  quotes Francis Quales: 'The vulgar Proverb's crost: he can hardly be a good Bowler and
  an Honest man' (*Emblemes* (1635), I, x).

13

bowler; but he makes a handsome figure, and rides in his coach, that he formerly used to ride behind. 130

AIMWELL

But did you observe poor Jack Generous in the park last week?

ARCHER

Yes, with his autumnal periwig shading his melancholy face, his coat older than anything but its fashion, with one hand idle in his pocket, and with the other picking his useless teeth; and though the Mall was crowded with company, yet was poor 135 Jack as single and solitary as a lion in a desert.

AIMWELL

And as much avoided, for no crime upon earth but the want of money.

ARCHER

And that's enough. Men must not be poor; idleness is the root of all evil; the world's wide enough, let 'em bustle. Fortune has 140 taken the weak under her protection, but men of sense are left to their industry.

AIMWELL

Upon which topic we proceed, and I think luckily hitherto. Would not any man swear now that I am a man of quality, and you my servant, when, if our intrinsic value were known – 145

ARCHER

Come, come, we are the men of intrinsic value, who can strike fortunes out of ourselves, whose worth is independent of accidents in life, or revolutions in government: we have heads to get money, and hearts to spend it.

---

130 *ride behind* See the note at ll. 7–8 above.

131 *the park* St James's Park

132 *periwig* the long curled wig (*perruque* in French) adopted by well-to-do men after the Restoration

135 *the Mall* a walk bordered by trees in St James Park

137 *want* lack; compare Prologue l. 21.

139–40 *idleness . . . evil* Archer, wittily justifying their stratagem, plays on the proverbial notion 'the Devil finds work for idle hands to do'. Compare Isaac Watts, *Divine Songs for Children* (1715): 'In works of labour, or of skill / I would be busy too; / For Satan still finds some mischief / For idle hands to do.'

140 *bustle* be vigorously active; compare Shakespeare's ambitious Richard of Gloucester: 'God take King Edward to his mercy, / And leave the world for me to bustle in!' (*Richard III*, I.i.152)

144 *quality* high rank; compare II.i.17, II.ii.69.

AIMWELL

As to our hearts, I grant ye, they are as willing tits as any   150
within twenty degrees; but I have no great opinion of our heads
from the service they have done us hitherto, unless it be that
they have brought us from London hither to Lichfield, made me
a lord, and you my servant.

ARCHER

That's more than you could expect already. But what money   155
have we left?

AIMWELL

But two hundred pound.

ARCHER

And our horses, clothes, rings, etc. Why, we have very good
fortunes now for moderate people; and let me tell you, that
this two hundred pound, besides the experience that we are   160
now masters of, is a better estate than the thousand we have
spent. – Our friends indeed began to suspect that our pockets
were low; but we came off with flying colours, showed no signs
of want either in word or deed.

AIMWELL

Ay, and our going to Brussels was a good pretence enough for   165
our sudden disappearing; and I warrant you, our friends
imagine that we are gone a-volunteering.

ARCHER

Why, faith, if this prospect fails, it must e'en come to that. I am
for venturing one of the hundreds, if you will, upon
this knight-errantry; but, in case it should fail, we'll reserve the   170

---

150 *tits* inferior horses, nags
159–162 *and . . . spent* ed. (and let me tell you, besides thousand, that this two hundred
pound, with the experience that we are now masters of, is a better estate that the ten we
have spent Q) This text adopts the emendation proposed for Q's nonsense by Alan
Roper ('How much did Farquhar's Beaux Spend in London?', *Studies in Bibliography*, 45
(1992), 105–112). After reviewing previous emendations, most moving 'thousand' after
'ten', Roper argues that 'besides' and 'thousand' are two separate Farquhar alterations
or substitutions, 'besides' replacing 'with', and 'thousand' 'ten'. Moreover, £10,000,
however neatly matching the value of the dowries of Mrs Sullen and Dorinda, is an
implausibly large amount for even two younger brothers to have spent.
165 *Brussels* The city had been captured by the English and their allies in 1706.
167 *a-volunteering* i.e. for the army; for this use of 'a-' as a preposition of action, compare
a-considering (l. 300), and many other instances throughout
170 *knight-errantry* speaking of their 'prospect' as the adventure of a wandering knight of
romance, e.g. Don Quixote; compare *knight-errants* (I.i.363).

t'other to carry us to some counterscarp, where we may die as we lived, in a blaze.

AIMWELL

With all my heart; and we have lived justly, Archer: we can't say we have spent our fortunes, but that we have enjoyed 'em.

ARCHER

Right, so much pleasure for so much money. We have had our   175
pennyworths, and had I millions, I would go to the same market
again. O London, London! Well, we have had our share, and let
us be thankful. Past pleasures, for aught I know, are best, such as
we are sure of; those to come may disappoint us.

AIMWELL

It has often grieved the heart of me to see how some inhuman   180
wretches murder their kind fortunes; those that, by sacrificing
all to one appetite, shall starve all the rest. – You shall have some
that live only in their palates, and in their sense of tasting shall
drown the other four. Others are only epicures in appearances,
such who shall starve their nights to make a figure a days, and   185
famish their own to feed the eyes of others. A contrary sort
confine their pleasures to the dark, and contract their spacious
acres to the circuit of a muff-string.

ARCHER

Right, but they find the Indies in that spot where they
consume 'em, and I think your kind keepers have much the   190
best on't, for they indulge the most senses by one expense.
There's the seeing, hearing, and feeling amply gratified; and
some philosophers will tell you, that from such a commerce
there arises a sixth sense, that gives infinitely more pleasure
than the other five put together.   195

---

171 *counterscarp* in fortification 'the outer wall, or slope of the ditch which supports the covered way' (Jeffares), and implying here, from Archer's next words, a place in the thick of the fighting

185 *a days* in the day time

188 *muff-string* i.e. a woman

189–90 *but . . . consume 'em* but they find treasure in the place where they spend their resources (with a sexual innuendo)

190 *kind keepers* men who maintain a woman in return for exclusive right to her sexual favours

194 *a sixth sense* an intuitive faculty capable of perceptions beyond the five senses; the term was recently adopted (*OED*'s first usage is 1678). Archer gives the phrase a sexual meaning.

AIMWELL

And to pass to the other extremity, of all keepers, I think those
the worst that keep their money.

ARCHER

Those are the most miserable wights in being; they destroy the
rights of nature, and disappoint the blessings of providence.
Give me a man that keeps his five senses keen and bright as his   200
sword, that has 'em always drawn out in their just order and
strength, with his reason as commander at the head of 'em, that
detaches 'em by turns upon whatever party of pleasure
agreeably offers, and commands 'em to retreat upon the least
appearance of disadvantage or danger. – For my part, I can stick   205
to my bottle, while my wine, my company, and my reason holds
good; I can be charmed with Sappho's singing without falling
in love with her face; I love hunting, but would not, like
Acteon, be eaten up by my own dogs; I love a fine house, but
let another keep it; and just so I love a fine woman.   210

AIMWELL

In that last particular you have the better of me.

ARCHER

Ay, you're such an amorous puppy, that I'm afraid you'll spoil
our sport; you can't counterfeit the passion without feeling it.

AIMWELL

Though the whining part be out of doors in town, 'tis still in

---

198 *wights* men
200–5 the first of Farquhar's many characteristic military metaphors; see p. xiv.
207 *Sappho* the Greek lyric poet, born in the seventh century BC, and here signifying a
   female singer or poet
209 *Acteon* the mythical hunter who came upon the goddess Diana, the virgin huntress,
   bathing, and was transformed by her into a stag; he fled, and was torn to pieces by his
   hounds
212–15 *Ay, you're . . . ladies* Included in *Love's Catechism*: Tom. *But what say you to those
   amorous Puppies that can't counterfeit the Passion of Love without feeling it?* Betty. *'Tis
   true, tho' the whining part be out of Doors in Town, yet 'tis in force with the Country
   Ladies.* (Kenny, II, 456).
214 *whining part* David S. Berkeley explains that in the late seventeenth century 'whining
   love' meant not just the tone of voice of the romantic lover but 'a definite and precise
   set of attitudes, posture and kind of eloquence', derived from French romances, and
   fashionable in literature and in certain social circles. See 'The Art of Whining love',
   Studies in Philology, 52 (1955), 478–96.
   out of doors out of fashion

force with the country ladies. – And let me tell you, Frank, the   215
fool in that passion shall outdo the knave at any time.

ARCHER

Well, I won't dispute it now; you command for the day, and so
I submit. – At Nottingham, you know, I am to be master.

AIMWELL

And at Lincoln, I again.

ARCHER

Then at Norwich I mount, which, I think, shall be our last stage;   220
for, if we fail there, we'll embark for Holland, bid adieu to
Venus, and welcome Mars.

AIMWELL

A match!

Enter BONNIFACE

Mum!

BONNIFACE

What will your worship please to have for supper?   225

AIMWELL

What have you got?

BONNIFACE

Sir, we have a delicate piece of beef in the pot, and a pig at the
fire.

AIMWELL

Good supper-meat, I must confess. – I can't eat beef,
landlord.   230

ARCHER

And I hate pig.

AIMWELL

Hold your prating, sirrah, do you know who you are?

BONNIFACE

Please to bespeak something else, I have everything in the
house.

AIMWELL

Have you any veal?   235

215–16 *the fool . . . knave* In cards, the joker will beat the knave (the jack).
221 *Holland* to join the allied army
229 *Good supper-meat* ironic, since supper, the last meal of the day, is usually less substantial
than dinner

BONNIFACE

Veal! Sir, we had a delicate loin of veal on Wednesday last.

AIMWELL

Have you got any fish or wildfowl?

BONNIFACE

As for fish, truly sir, we are an inland town, and indifferently
provided with fish, that's the truth on't, and then for wildfowl,
– we have a delicate couple of rabbits.   240

AIMWELL

Get me the rabbits fricasseed.

BONNIFACE

Fricasseed! Lard, sir, they'll eat much better smothered with
onions.

ARCHER

Pshaw! Damn your onions!

AIMWELL

Again, sirrah! – Well, landlord, what you please. But hold, I have   245
a small charge of money, and your house is so full of strangers
that I believe it may be safer in your custody than mine; for
when this fellow of mine gets drunk, he minds nothing. – Here,
sirrah, reach me the strong-box.

ARCHER

Yes, sir. – (*Aside*) This will give us a reputation.   *Brings the box*   250

AIMWELL

Here, landlord, the locks are sealed down both for your security
and mine. It holds somewhat above two hundred pound: if you
doubt it, I'll count it to you after supper; but be sure you lay it
where I may have it at a minute's warning, for my affairs are a
little dubious at present; perhaps I may be gone in half an hour,   255
perhaps I may be your guest till the best part of that be spent;
and pray order your ostler to keep my horses always saddled.
But one thing above the rest I must beg, that you would let this
fellow have none of your *Anno Domini*, as you call it, – for
he's the most insufferable sot. – Here, sirrah, light me to my   260
chamber.

Exit, lighted by ARCHER

241 *fricasseed* cut into pieces and served in a sauce
246 *charge of money* amount of money
261 s.d. *lighted by* Archer picks up a candlestick; in V.ii, another night scene, the s.d. mentions *lights*, i.e. candles.

BONNIFACE

Cherry, daughter Cherry!

Enter CHERRY

CHERRY

D'ye call, Father?

BONNIFACE

Ay, child, you must lay by this box for the gentleman, 'tis full of
money.   265

CHERRY

Money! All that money! Why sure, father, the gentleman comes
to be chosen parliament-man. Who is he?

BONNIFACE

I don't know what to make of him; he talks of keeping his
horses ready saddled, and of going perhaps at a minute's
warning, or of staying perhaps till the best part of this be spent.   270

CHERRY

Ay, ten to one, father, he's a highwayman.

BONNIFACE

A highwayman! Upon my life, girl, you have hit it, and this box
is some new-purchased booty. – Now, could we find him out,
the money were ours.

CHERRY

He don't belong to our gang.   275

BONNIFACE

What horses have they?

CHERRY

The master rides upon a black.

BONNIFACE

A black! Ten to one, the man upon the black mare; and since he
don't belong to our fraternity, we may betray him with a safe
conscience; I don't think it lawful to harbour any rogues but   280
mine own. – Look ye, child, as the saying is, we must go
cunningly to work. Proofs we must have. The gentleman's
servant loves to drink, I'll ply him that way, and ten to one loves
a wench; you must work him t'other way.

267 *parliament-man* Bribery of the electors with money or drink was and continued long to
be common practice in parliamentary elections.
273 *new-purchased* recently taken

CHERRY

Father, would you have me give my secret for his?   285

BONNIFACE

Consider, child, there's two hundred pound to boot. (*Ringing without*) Coming, coming. – Child, mind your business. [*Exit*]

CHERRY

What a rogue is my father! My father! I deny it. – My mother was a good, generous, free-hearted woman, and I can't tell how far her good nature might have extended for the good of her   290 children. This landlord of mine, for I think I can call him no more, would betray his guest, and debauch his daughter into the bargain – by a footman too!

Enter ARCHER

ARCHER

What footman, pray, mistress, is so happy as to be the subject of your contemplation?   295

CHERRY

Whoever he is, friend, he'll be but little the better for't.

ARCHER

I hope so, for I'm sure you did not think of me.

CHERRY

Suppose I had?

ARCHER

Why then you're but even with me; for the minute I came in, I was a-considering in what manner I should make love to you.   300

CHERRY

Love to me, friend!

ARCHER

Yes, child.

CHERRY

Child! Manners! If you kept a little more distance, friend, it would become you much better.

ARCHER

Distance! Good night, sauce-box.   *Going*   305

285 *secret* with a sexual innuendo
286 *to boot* in addition
287 *business* a pun: 'the slang meaning of "business" was "sexual intercourse" ' (Cordner)

21

CHERRY

A pretty fellow! I like his pride. – Sir, pray sir, you see, sir. (ARCHER *returns*) I have the credit to be entrusted with your master's fortune here, which sets me a degree above his footman; I hope, sir, you an't affronted.

ARCHER

Let me look you full in the face, and I'll tell you whether you   310
can affront me or no. – 'Sdeath, child, you have a pair of delicate eyes, and you don't know what to do with 'em.

CHERRY

Why, sir, don't I see everybody?

ARCHER

Ay, but if some women had 'em, they would kill everybody. – Prithee, instruct me; I would fain make love to you, but I don't   315
know what to say.

CHERRY

Why, did you never make love to anybody before?

ARCHER

Never to a person of your figure, I can assure you, madam: my addresses have always been confined to people within my own sphere; I never aspired so high before.   *A song*   320

But you look so bright
And are dressed so tight,
That a man would swear you're right,
As arm was e'er laid over.
Such an air   325
You freely wear
To ensnare,
As makes each guest a lover:

Since then, my dear, I'm your guest,
Prithee give me of the best   330
Of what is ready dressed:
Since then, my dear, etc.

311–13 *S'death . . . everybody?* Included in *Love's Catechism*: Tom. *S'death, Betty, you have a pair of delicate Eyes, pray what d'ye do with'm? Betty. Why, Tom, don't I see every Body? Tom. Ay, but if some women had 'em, they wou'd kill every body.* (Kenny, II, 456).
321–32 1728 (But you look . . . tight, &. Q)

CHERRY

(*Aside*) What can I think of this man? – Will you give me that
song, sir?

ARCHER

Ay, my dear, take it while 'tis warm. (*Kisses her*) Death and fire!   335
Her lips are honeycombs.

CHERRY

And I wish there had been bees too, to have stung you for your
impudence.

ARCHER

There's a swarm of Cupids, my little Venus, that has done the
business much better.   340

CHERRY

(*Aside*) This fellow is misbegotten as well as I. – What's your
name, sir?

ARCHER

Name! (*Aside*) Egad, I have forgot it. – O! Martin.

CHERRY

Where were you born?

ARCHER

In St. Martin's parish.   345

CHERRY

What was your father?

ARCHER

St. Martin's parish.

CHERRY

Then, friend, good night.

ARCHER

I hope not.

CHERRY

You may depend upon't.   350

ARCHER

Upon what?

CHERRY

That you're very impudent.

ARCHER

That you're very handsome.

341 *misbegotten* here in a positive sense: of higher birth than his present occupation suggests

CHERRY
That you're a footman.
ARCHER
That you're an angel.   355
CHERRY
I shall be rude.
ARCHER
So shall I.
CHERRY
Let go my hand.
ARCHER
Give me a kiss.   *Kisses her*

Call without Cherry, Cherry!

CHERRY
I'mm – my father calls. You plaguy devil, how durst you stop   360
my breath so? – Offer to follow me one step, if you dare. [*Exit*]
ARCHER
A fair challenge, by this light! This is a pretty fair opening of
an adventure: but we are knight-errants, and so Fortune be our
guide.   *Exit*

ACT II. [SCENE i]

Scene, a gallery in LADY BOUNTIFUL's *house*

[*Enter*] MRS SULLEN *and* DORINDA, *meeting*

DORINDA
Morrow, my dear sister. Are you for church this morning?
MRS SULLEN
Anywhere to pray, for Heaven alone can help me. But I think,

---

356 *I shall be rude* 'That you're a devil' would complete the pattern; instead Cherry substitutes this phrase.
363 *knight-errants* See note at I.i.170.
364 Q adds: '*The End of the First Act*'
  0 s.d. 1 *gallery* a long upstairs room hung with pictures

Dorinda, there's no form of prayer in the liturgy against bad
husbands.

DORINDA

But there's a form of law in Doctors' Commons, and I swear,   5
sister Sullen, rather than see you thus continually discontented,
I would advise you to apply to that. For besides the part that I
bear in your vexatious broils, as being sister to the husband and
friend to the wife, your example gives me such an impression of
matrimony, that I shall be apt to condemn my person to a long   10
vacation all its life. – But supposing, madam, that you brought
it to a case of separation, what can you urge against your
husband? My brother is, first, the most constant man alive.

MRS SULLEN

The most constant husband, I grant ye.

DORINDA

He never sleeps from you.   15

MRS SULLEN

No, he always sleeps with me.

DORINDA

He allows you a maintenance suitable to your quality.

MRS SULLEN

A maintenance! Do you take me, madam, for an hospital child,
that I must sit down and bless my benefactors for meat, drink,
and clothes? As I take it, madam, I brought your brother   20
ten thousand pounds, out of which I might expect some pretty
things, called pleasures.

DORINDA

You share in all the pleasures that the country affords.

MRS SULLEN

Country pleasures! Racks and torments! Dost think, child, that

---

5 *Doctors' Commons* The College of the Doctors of Civil Law in London: lawyers practicing
   there dealt with marriage-licences, divorce and wills. The court was dissolved in 1857.

8 *broils* quarrels

10–11 *to condemn . . . life* i.e. her horror of matrimony will make her ready to condemn her
   body ('person') to life-long inactivity ('vacation'), by which Dorinda means no sex and
   no childbearing

   long vacation the period in the summer when the courts did not sit

18 *an hospital child* a pauper brought up in a charitable institution; *an hospital* words of
   French origin with initial 'h' were until the nineteenth century pronounced as in French
   with a silent h and so took the *an* form of the indefinite article.

my limbs were made for leaping of ditches, and clambering over 25
stiles; or that my parents, wisely foreseeing my future happiness
in country pleasures, had early instructed me in the rural
accomplishments of drinking fat ale, playing at whisk, and
smoking tobacco with my husband; or of spreading of plasters,
brewing of diet-drinks, and stilling rosemary water, with the 30
good old gentlewoman, my mother-in-law?

DORINDA

I'm sorry, madam, that it is not more in our power to divert
you. I could wish indeed that our entertainments were a little
more polite, or your taste a little less refined. But, pray, madam,
how came the poets and philosophers, that laboured so much in 35
hunting after pleasure, to place it at last in a country life?

MRS SULLEN

Because they wanted money, child, to find out the pleasures of
the town. Did you ever see a poet or philosopher worth ten
thousand pound? If you can show me such a man, I'll lay
you fifty pound you'll find him somewhere within the weekly 40
bills. – Not that I disapprove rural pleasures, as the poets
have painted them. In their landscape every Phyllis has her
Corydon, every murmuring stream, and every flowery mead
gives fresh alarms to love. – Besides, you'll find that their
couples were never married. – But yonder I see my Corydon, 45
and a sweet swain it is, Heaven knows. – Come, Dorinda, don't
be angry; he's my husband, and your brother, and between
both, is he not a sad brute?

DORINDA

I have nothing to say to your part of him, you're the best judge.

28 *fat ale* full-bodied ale
29 *plasters* ed. (plaisters Q, an obsolete form)
30 *diet-drinks* medicinal drinks
   stilling distilling
40–41 *within the weekly bills* i.e. in London. Beginning in 1592, the London Company of
   Parish Clerks published an official list of deaths, and parishes contributing to this weekly
   tally constituted the area 'within the weekly bills'.
42–3 *Phyllis . . . Corydon* common names for figures in pastoral poetry and romance
43 *murmuring stream . . . flowery mead . . . to love* the conventional language of pastoral
46 *swain* Mrs Sullen plays on 'swain' meaning both a lover in pastoral poetry, and a country
   labourer.

MRS SULLEN

O sister, sister! If ever you marry, beware of a sullen, silent sot, 50
one that's always musing, but never thinks. – There's some
diversion in a talking blockhead; and since a woman must
wear chains, I would have the pleasure of hearing 'em rattle a
little. – Now you shall see, but take this by the way. – He came
home this morning at his usual hour of four, wakened me out 55
of a sweet dream of something else by tumbling over the tea-
table, which he broke all to pieces. After his man and he had
rolled about the room like sick passengers in a storm, he comes
flounce into bed, dead as a salmon into a fishmonger's basket,
his feet cold as ice, his breath hot as a furnace, and his hands 60
and his face as greasy as his flannel nightcap. – O matrimony! –
He tosses up the clothes with a barbarous swing over his
shoulders, disorders the whole economy of my bed, leaves me
half naked, and my whole night's comfort is the tuneable
serenade of that wakeful nightingale, his nose. – O the pleasure 65
of counting the melancholy clock by a snoring husband! – But
now, sister, you shall see how handsomely, being a well-bred
man, he will beg my pardon.

Enter SULLEN

SULLEN

My head aches consumedly.

MRS SULLEN

Will you be pleased, my dear, to drink tea with us this morning? 70
It may do your head good.

SULLEN

No.

50–54 *If ever . . . little* Included in *Love's Catechism*: Betty begins: '*O by no means; for if ever I
marry, I'll beware of a sullen, silent Fool,*' with the rest identical.
52–3 *a woman must wear chains* Early feminists compared married women to slaves. Mary
Astell wrote: 'Women are not so well united as to form an Insurrection. They are for the
most part Wise enough to Love their Chains', 'Preface', *Reflections upon Marriage*, 1706,
in *The First English Feminist*, ed. Bridget Hill (Aldershot 1986), p. 86.
59 *flounce* 'with a sudden jerk or flop' (*OED*, quoting this line)
63 *economy* orderly arrangement; applying the term to her bed is another instance of Mrs
Sullen's wit.
64 *tuneable* tuneful
69 *consumedly* confoundedly, the play's low expletive, used by Scrub as well as Sullen, and
see the note below at II.ii.97

DORINDA
Coffee, brother?

SULLEN
Pshaw!

MRS SULLEN
Will you please to dress and go to church with me? The air may   75
help you.

SULLEN
Scrub.

Enter SCRUB

SCRUB
Sir.

SULLEN
What day o'th week is this?

SCRUB
Sunday, an't please your worship.   80

SULLEN
Sunday! Bring me a dram, and d'ye hear, set out the venison-
pasty and a tankard of strong beer upon the hall-table. I'll go
to breakfast.   *Going*

DORINDA
Stay, stay, brother, you shan't get off so. You were very naught
last night, and must make your wife reparation. Come, come,   85
brother, won't you ask pardon?

SULLEN
For what?

DORINDA
For being drunk last night.

SULLEN
I can afford it, can't I?

MRS SULLEN
But I can't, sir.   90

SULLEN
Then you may let it alone.

MRS SULLEN
But I must tell you, sir, that this is not to be borne.

80 *an't* and it; also at IV.i.24; elsewhere *an't* is either colloquial 'aren't, or 'am not'
84 *naught* bad, wicked

SULLEN

I'm glad on't.

MRS SULLEN

What is the reason, sir, that you use me thus inhumanly?

SULLEN

Scrub.   95

SCRUB

Sir.

SULLEN

Get things ready to shave my head.   *Exit*

MRS SULLEN

Have a care of coming near his temples, Scrub, for fear you meet something there that may turn the edge of your razor.

[*Exit* SCRUB]

– Inveterate stupidity! Did you ever know so hard, so obstinate   100
a spleen as his? O sister, sister! I shall never ha' good of the beast till I get him to town. London, dear London, is the place for managing and breaking a husband.

DORINDA

And has not a husband the same opportunities there for humbling a wife?   105

MRS SULLEN

No, no, child, 'tis a standing maxim in conjugal discipline that when a man would enslave his wife, he hurries her into the country; and when a lady would be arbitrary with her husband, she wheedles her booby up to town. – A man dare

---

94 *inhumanly* ed. (inhumanely Q) The two spellings did not as now indicate different meanings; since Mrs Sullen stresses her husband's beast-like qualities, inhuman suits better.

97 *shave my head* Men shaved their heads so their wigs fitted tightly. 'I find the convenience of Perrywigs is so great that I have cut off all short again, and will keep to periwigs.' (Samuel Pepys, *Diary*, 22 May 1665, qtd. in Claire Tomalin, *Samuel Pepys: The Unequalled Self* (2002), p. 197.)

99 *something there* referring to the cuckold's horns: one of Mrs Sullen's risqué remarks

101 *spleen* Literally an organ in the body, it was a fashionable term for a host of conditions, bad temper, ennui, malaise, depression, in both men and women. In *The Rape of the Lock* (1714) Pope mocks this affectation in the Cave of Spleen episode (Canto four). See also the note at III.iii.126.

108 *arbitrary* despotic, tyrannical

109 *booby* 'a dull heavy stupid fellow' (Johnson's *Dictionary*)

not play the tyrant in London because there are so many 110
examples to encourage the subject to rebel. O Dorinda,
Dorinda! A fine woman may do anything in London. O'my
conscience, she may raise an army of forty thousand men.

DORINDA

I fancy, sister, you have a mind to be trying your power that
way here in Lichfield. You have drawn the French count to your 115
colours already.

MRS SULLEN

The French are a people that can't live without their
gallantries.

DORINDA

And some English that I know, sister, are not averse to such
amusements. 120

MRS SULLEN

Well, sister, since the truth will out, it may do as well now as
hereafter. I think one way to rouse my lethargic, sottish husband
is to give him a rival. Security begets negligence in all people,
and men must be alarmed to make 'em alert in their duty.
Women are like pictures: of no value in the hands of a fool till 125
he hears men of sense bid high for the purchase.

DORINDA

This might do, sister, if my brother's understanding were to be
convinced into a passion for you; but I fancy there's a natural
aversion of his side, and I fancy, sister, that you don't come
much behind him, if you dealt fairly. 130

MRS SULLEN

I own it, we are united contradictions, fire and water. But I
could be contented, with a great many other wives, to humour
the censorious mob, and give the world an appearance of
living well with my husband, could I bring him but to dissemble
a little kindness to keep me in countenance. 135

DORINDA

But how do you know, sister, but that instead of rousing your
husband by this artifice to a counterfeit kindness, he should
awake in a real fury?

115–16 *to your colours* Figuratively, to enlist in her regiment: in Farquhar women as well as
men use military metaphors.
133 *mob* the common people

MRS SULLEN

Let him. – If I can't entice him to the one, I would provoke him
to the other.   140

DORINDA

But how must I behave myself between ye?

MRS SULLEN

You must assist me.

DORINDA

What, against my own brother!

MRS SULLEN

He's but half a brother, and I'm your entire friend. If I go a
step beyond the bounds of honour, leave me; till then, I expect   145
you should go along with me in everything. While I trust my
honour in your hands, you may trust your brother's in mine. –
The count is to dine here today.

DORINDA

'Tis a strange thing, sister, that I can't like that man.

MRS SULLEN

You like nothing, your time is not come. Love and death have   150
their fatalities, and strike home one time or other. – You'll pay
for all one day, I warrant ye. – But come, my lady's tea is ready,
and 'tis almost church time.   *Exeunt*

[ACT II. SCENE ii]

Scene, the inn

Enter AIMWELL *dressed, and* ARCHER

AIMWELL

And was she the daughter of the house?

ARCHER

The landlord is so blind as to think so; but I dare swear she has
better blood in her veins.

144 *half a brother* He is her step-brother.
152 *tea is ready* 'Ten, about the hour of tea-drinking throughout the kingdom.' (*The Recruit-
     ing Officer*, IV.ii.272, where the editor notes: 'Tea was expensive (16s. to 18s. a pound in
     1706) and the tea-table an established female institution.'
  0 s.d. 2 *dressed* i.e. in day clothes, not in a night gown; Compare V.ii.0 s.d. 2 *undressed*

AIMWELL

Why dost think so?

ARCHER

Because the baggage has a pert *je ne sais quoi*; she reads plays,   5
keeps a monkey, and is troubled with vapours.

AIMWELL

By which discoveries I guess that you know more of her.

ARCHER

Not yet, faith. The lady gives herself airs, forsooth, nothing
under a gentleman.

AIMWELL

Let me take her in hand.   10

ARCHER

Say one word more o'that, and I'll declare myself, spoil your
sport there, and everywhere else. Look ye, Aimwell, every man
in his own sphere.

AIMWELL

Right, and therefore you must pimp for your master.

ARCHER

In the usual forms, good sir, after I have served myself. – But to   15
our business. – You are so well dressed, Tom, and make so
handsome a figure, that I fancy you may do execution in a
country church; the exterior part strikes first, and you're in the
right to make that impression favourable.

AIMWELL

There's something in that which may turn to advantage. The   20
appearance of a stranger in a country church draws as many
gazers as a blazing star; no sooner he comes into the cathedral
but a chain of whispers runs buzzing round the congregation in
a moment. – Who is he? Whence comes he? Do you know him?
– Then I, sir, tips me the verger with half a crown. He pockets   25
the simony, and inducts me into the best pew in the church.

---

5 *je ne sais quoi* 'a certain something' (French)
6 *keeps a monkey* a fashionable pet; an obvious parallel is in Rochester's poem, 'A Letter
   from Artemisa in the Town, to Chloe in the Country', where a lady embraces her
   pet monkey, the 'dirty chatt'ring monster': 'Kiss me! thou curious miniature of man, /
   How odd thou art, how pretty! how Japan!'
   vapours common expression for low spirits, fainting, etc., especially in women of the
   upper classes, once believed to be produced by internal 'exhalations'
25 *verger* attendant in a church, church caretaker
26 *simony* the verger's tip; originally money paid to obtain a church office

I pull out my snuff-box, turn myself round, bow to the bishop,
or the dean, if he be the commanding officer, single out a
beauty, rivet both my eyes to hers, set my nose a-bleeding by
the strength of imagination, and show the whole church my   30
concern by my endeavouring to hide it. After the sermon the
whole town gives me to her for a lover, and by persuading the
lady that I am a-dying for her, the tables are turned, and she in
good earnest falls in love with me.

ARCHER

There's nothing in this, Tom, without a precedent; but instead   35
of riveting your eyes to a beauty, try to fix 'em upon a fortune,
that's our business at present.

AIMWELL

Pshaw, no woman can be a beauty without a fortune. – Let me
alone, for I am a marksman.

ARCHER

Tom.   40

AIMWELL

Ay.

ARCHER

When were you at church before, pray?

AIMWELL

Um – I was there at the coronation.

ARCHER

And how can you expect a blessing by going to church now?

AIMWELL

Blessing! Nay, Frank, I ask but for a wife.   *Exit*   45

ARCHER

Truly, the man is not very unreasonable in his demands.

Exit at the opposite door

Enter BONNIFACE *and* CHERRY

BONNIFACE

Well, daughter, as the saying is, have you brought Martin to
confess?

---

38 *Pshaw* post-Restoration expression of contempt or disgust
39 *marksman* you have a good eye, i.e. you aim well, the pun on his name is taken up again
in III.ii.1–3.
43 *coronation* of Queen Anne, April, 1702

CHERRY

Pray, father, don't put me upon getting anything out of a man. I'm but young, you know, father, and I don't understand wheedling. 50

BONIFACE

Young! Why you jade, as the saying is, can any woman wheedle that is not young? Your mother was useless at five and twenty. Not wheedle! Would you make your mother a whore, and me a cuckold, as the saying is? I tell you, his silence confesses it, and 55 his master spends his money so freely, and is so much a gentleman every manner of way that he must be a highwayman.

Enter GIBBET *in a cloak*

GIBBET

Landlord, landlord, is the coast clear?

BONIFACE

O Mr Gibbet, what's the news?

GIBBET

No matter, ask no questions, all fair and honourable. Here, my 60 dear Cherry. (*Gives her a bag*) Two hundred sterling pounds, as good as any that ever hanged or saved a rogue. Lay 'em by with the rest, and here – three wedding, or mourning rings, 'tis much the same you know. – Here, two silver-hilted swords. I took those from fellows that never show any part of their swords but 65 the hilts. Here is a diamond necklace which the lady hid in the privatest place in the coach, but I found it out. This gold watch I took from a pawnbroker's wife. It was left in her hands by a person of quality, there's the arms upon the case.

CHERRY

But who had you the money from? 70

GIBBET

Ah, poor woman! I pitied her. – From a poor lady just eloped from her husband. She had made up her cargo, and was bound for Ireland, as hard as she could drive. She told me of her husband's barbarous usage, and so I left her half a crown. But I had almost forgot, my dear Cherry, I have a present for you. 75

54–5 *Would . . . cuckold* i.e. you're no child of your parents if you can't wheedle
57 s.d. *GIBBET* originally, the gallows, and later a post with a projecting arm on which the bodies of criminals were hung in chains after their execution

CHERRY
What is't?

GIBBET
A pot of ceruse, my child, that I took out of a lady's under-pocket.

CHERRY
What, Mr Gibbet, do you think that I paint?

GIBBET
Why you jade, your betters do. I'm sure the lady that I took it   80
from had a coronet upon her handkerchief. – Here, take my
cloak, and go secure the premises.

CHERRY
I will secure 'em.   *Exit*

BONNIFACE
But, hark ye, where's Hounslow and Bagshot?

GIBBET
They'll be here tonight.   85

BONNIFACE
D'ye know of any other gentlemen o'the pad on this road?

GIBBET
No.

BONNIFACE
I fancy that I have two that lodge in the house just now.

GIBBET
The devil! How d'ye smoke 'em?

BONNIFACE
Why, the one is gone to church.   90

GIBBET
That's suspicious, I must confess.

BONNIFACE
And the other is now in his master's chamber. He pretends
to be servant to the other; we'll call him out and pump him a
little.

GIBBET
With all my heart.   95

77 *ceruse* a white cosmetic paint
81 *coronet* marking her noble rank: peers (i.e. the nobility) are entitled to wear a small crown
86 *gentlemen o'the pad* slang for highwaymen
89 *smoke* suspect

BONNIFACE
Mr Martin, Mr Martin!

Enter ARCHER *combing a periwig, and singing*

GIBBET
The roads are consumed deep. I'm as dirty as old Brentford
at Christmas. – A good pretty fellow, that. Whose servant are
you, friend?

ARCHER
My master's.   100

GIBBET
Really?

ARCHER
Really.

GIBBET
[*Aside*] That's much. – The fellow has been at the bar by his
evasions. – But, pray sir, what is your master's name?

ARCHER
Tall, all dall. – (*Sings, and combs the periwig*) This is the most   105
obstinate curl –

GIBBET
I ask you his name.

ARCHER
Name, sir, – *Tall, all dall* – I never asked him his name in my life.
Tall, all dall.

BONNIFACE
What think you now?   110

GIBBET
Plain, plain, he talks now as if he were before a judge. – But,
pray friend, which way does your master travel?

ARCHER
A-horseback.

GIBBET
Very well again, an old offender, right. – But I mean, does he go
upwards or downwards?   115

---

96   s.d *ARCHER* 1728 (Martin Q)
97   *consumed* confounded; and see the note at II.i.69.
     Brentford on the Thames in Middlesex
115 *upwards or downwards* towards or away from London. Archer replies figuratively, their
     fortunes are sinking; Gibbet alludes to his fear of being hanged.

ARCHER

Downwards, I fear, sir. *Tall, all.*

GIBBET

I'm afraid my fate will be a contrary way.

BONNIFACE

Ha, ha, ha! Mr Martin, you're very arch. – This gentleman is
only travelling towards Chester, and would be glad of your
company, that's all. – Come, captain, you'll stay tonight, I   120
suppose. I'll show you a chamber. – Come, captain.

GIBBET

Farewell, friend –

Exeunt

ARCHER

Captain, your servant. – Captain! A pretty fellow. 'Sdeath, I
wonder that the officers of the army don't conspire to beat all
scoundrels in red but their own.   125

Enter CHERRY

CHERRY

(*Aside*) Gone, and Martin here! I hope he did not listen. I
would have the merit of the discovery all my own, because
I would oblige him to love me. – Mr Martin, who was that man
with my father?

ARCHER

Some recruiting sergeant, or whipped-out trooper, I suppose.   130

CHERRY

All's safe, I find.

ARCHER

Come, my dear, have you conned over the catechise I taught you
last night?

CHERRY

Come, question me.

118 *arch* crafty, roguish
122 s.d. *Exeunt* ed. (*Exit* Q) They leave together.
130 *recruiting sergeant* a joke between Farquhar and the audience, recalling his most recent
     play, *The Recruiting Officer*
     whipped-out flogged and then dismissed from the army; *trooper* horse soldier

ARCHER

What is love? 135

CHERRY

Love is I know not what, it comes I know not how, and goes I know not when.

ARCHER

Very well, an apt scholar. (*Chucks her under the chin*) Where does love enter?

CHERRY

Into the eyes. 140

ARCHER

And where go out?

CHERRY

I won't tell ye.

ARCHER

What are objects of that passion?

CHERRY

Youth, beauty, and clean linen.

ARCHER

The reason? 145

CHERRY

The first two are fashionable in nature, and the third at court.

ARCHER

That's my dear. What are the signs and tokens of that passion?

CHERRY

A stealing look, a stammering tongue, words improbable, designs impossible, and actions impracticable. 150

ARCHER

That's my good child, kiss me. – What must a lover do to obtain his mistress?

CHERRY

He must adore the person that disdains him, he must bribe the chambermaid that betrays him, and court the footman that laughs at him. – He must, he must – 155

ARCHER

Nay, child, I must whip you if you don't mind your lesson. He must treat his –

135–71 All of Cherry and Archer's catechism reappears in *Love's Catechism*.

CHERRY

O, ay, he must treat his enemies with respect, his friends with
indifference, and all the world with contempt; he must suffer
much, and fear more; he must desire much and hope little; in   160
short, he must embrace his ruin, and throw himself away.

ARCHER

Had ever man so hopeful a pupil as mine? Come, my dear, why
is love called a riddle?

CHERRY

Because, being blind, he leads those that see, and, though a
child, he governs a man.   165

ARCHER

Mighty well! – And why is love pictured blind?

CHERRY

Because the painters, out of the weakness or privilege of their
art, chose to hide those eyes that they could not draw.

ARCHER

That's my dear little scholar, kiss me again. – And why should
love, that's a child, govern a man?   170

CHERRY

Because that a child is the end of love.

ARCHER

And so ends love's catechism. – And now, my dear, we'll go in
and make my master's bed.

CHERRY

Hold, hold, Mr Martin. – You have taken a great deal of pains to
instruct me, and what d'ye think I have learned by it?   175

ARCHER

What?

CHERRY

That your discourse and your habit are contradictions, and it
would be nonsense in me to believe you a footman any longer.

ARCHER

'Oons, what a witch it is!

CHERRY

Depend upon this, sir: nothing in this garb shall ever tempt me, 180
for though I was born to servitude, I hate it. – Own your
condition, swear you love me, and then –

179 *'Oons* by God's wounds, a mild oath frequent in the play
182 *condition* rank, social position

ARCHER
And then we shall go make the bed?
CHERRY
Yes.
ARCHER
You must know then, that I am born a gentleman, my education   185
was liberal; but I went to London a younger brother, fell into
the hands of sharpers who stripped me of my money. My
friends disowned me, and now my necessity brings me to what
you see.
CHERRY
Then take my hand – promise to marry me before you sleep,   190
and I'll make you master of two thousand pound.
ARCHER
How?
CHERRY
Two thousand pound that I have this minute in my own
custody. So throw off your livery this instant, and I'll go find a
parson.   195
ARCHER
What said you? A parson!
CHERRY
What! Do you scruple?
ARCHER
Scruple! No, no, but – two thousand pound you say?
CHERRY
And better.
ARCHER
'Sdeath, what shall I do? – But hark'ee, child, what need you   200
make me master of yourself and money, when you may have the
same pleasure out of me, and still keep your fortune in your
hands?
CHERRY
Then you won't marry me?
ARCHER
I would marry you, but –   205

187   *sharpers* swindlers, crooks
197   *scruple* hesitate, take exception

CHERRY

O sweet sir, I'm your humble servant. You're fairly caught.
Would you persuade me that any gentleman who could bear the
scandal of wearing a livery, would refuse two thousand pound,
let the condition be what it would? – No, no, sir. – But I hope
you'll pardon the freedom I have taken, since it was only to 210
inform myself of the respect that I ought to pay you.   *Going*

ARCHER

Fairly bit, by Jupiter! – Hold, hold, and have you actually two
thousand pound?

CHERRY

Sir, I have my secrets as well as you. – When you please to be
more open, I shall be more free, and be assured that I have 215
discoveries that will match yours, be what they will. – In the
meanwhile, be satisfied that no discovery I make shall ever hurt
you, but beware of my father!   [*Exit*]

ARCHER

So – we're like to have as many adventures in our inn as Don
Quixote had in his. – Let me see – two thousand pound! If the 220
wench would promise to die when the money were spent, egad,
one would marry her, but the fortune may go off in a year or
two, and the wife may live – Lord knows how long! Then, an
innkeeper's daughter! Ay, that's the devil – there my pride
brings me off.   225

   For whatsoe'er the sages charge on pride,

   The angels' fall, and twenty faults beside,

   On earth I'm sure, 'mong us of mortal calling,

   Pride saves man oft, and woman too from falling.   *Exit*

206–9 *O sweet sir . . . would* Cherry mistakenly believes she has proved that Martin is not a
gentleman: she believes no gentleman reduced to being a footman would miss the
chance to marry two thousand pounds.

219–20 *adventures . . . Don Quixote* Cervantes' novel, published in English in 1612, was
widely read, and influential. Thomas Durfey's three-part *Comical History of Don
Quixote* (1694–5) dramatized episodes from the novel, and a one-play adaptation of
Durfey's work was still regularly performed in the 1730s. For similar allusions see, for
instance, Vanbrugh's *The Provoked Wife*, 'knight-errantry' III.i, 'Don Quixote', 'Sancho,
my squire' IV.i; for the novel's possible influence on this play see p. xiii, and for its
wider literary influence, see Ronald Paulson, *Don Quixote in England: The Aesthetics of
Laughter* (Baltimore, 1998).

229 Q adds: '*End of the Second Act*'

ACT III. [SCENE i]

Scene, LADY BOUNTIFUL'*s house*

Enter MRS SULLEN, DORINDA

MRS SULLEN

Ha, ha, ha, my dear sister, let me embrace thee, now we are friends indeed, for I shall have a secret of yours as a pledge for mine. – Now you'll be good for something, I shall have you conversable in the subjects of the sex.

DORINDA

But do you think I am so weak as to fall in love with a fellow at   5
first sight?

MRS SULLEN

Pshaw! Now you spoil all; why should not we be as free in our friendships as the men? I warrant you the gentleman has got to his confidant already, has avowed his passion, toasted your health, called you ten thousand angels, has run over your lips,   10
eyes, neck, shape, air and everything, in a description that warms their mirth to a second enjoyment.

DORINDA

Your hand, sister, I an't well.

MRS SULLEN

So, – she's breeding already – come child, up with it – hem a little – so – now tell me, don't you like the gentleman that we   15
saw at church just now?

DORINDA

The man's well enough.

MRS SULLEN

Well enough! Is he not a demi-god, a Narcissus, a star, the man i'the moon?

0 s.d. 1 LADY BOUNTIFUL'*s house* 1728 (*Scene continues* Q)
4 *subjects of the sex* matters that women talk about (i.e. love affairs)
5–12 *do you . . . enjoyment* included in *Love's Catechism* except for *why should . . . men?* and with a variation in ll. 8–9: *the gentleman . . . already* Q ('I warrant you the young whipster has got to some of his boon companions already *Love's Catechism*) In *Love's Catechism* the speaker is male (Tom).
7 *free* open
18 *Narcissus* the beautiful youth in Greek mythology who rejects the love of Echo, and is punished by falling in love with his own reflection in a lake, and drowning when he tries to embrace it

DORINDA

    O sister, I'm extremely ill.   20

MRS SULLEN

    Shall I send to your mother, child, for a little of her cephalic
    plaster to put on the soles of your feet, or shall I send to the
    gentleman for something for you? – Come, unlace your stays,
    unbosom yourself – the man is perfectly a pretty fellow, I saw
    him when he first came into church.   25

DORINDA

    I saw him too, sister, and with an air that shone methought like
    rays about his person.

MRS SULLEN

    Well said, up with it.

DORINDA

    No forward coquette behaviour, no airs to set him off, no
    studied looks nor artificial posture, – but nature did it all –   30

MRS SULLEN

    Better and better – one touch more – come.

DORINDA

    But then his looks – did you observe his eyes?

MRS SULLEN

    Yes, yes, I did – his eyes, well, what of his eyes?

DORINDA

    Sprightly, but not wandering; they seemed to view, but never
    gazed on anything but me – and then his looks so humble were,   35
    and yet so noble, that they aimed to tell me that he could with
    pride die at my feet, though he scorned slavery anywhere else.

MRS SULLEN

    The physic works purely. – How d'ye find yourself now, my
    dear?

DORINDA

    Hem! Much better, my dear. – O here comes our Mercury!   40

Enter SCRUB

Well, Scrub, what news of the gentleman?

21–2 *cephalic plaster* a plaster for the head. Mrs Sullen pretends to treat a young woman
    'head over heels' in love.
38 *physic* medicine; *works purely* really works
40 *Mercury* the messenger of the Gods

SCRUB

Madam, I have brought you a packet of news.

DORINDA

Open it quickly, come.

SCRUB

In the first place I enquired who the gentleman was. They told
me he was a stranger. Secondly, I asked what the gentleman was,   45
they answered and said, that they never saw him before. Thirdly,
I enquired what countryman he was, they replied 'twas more
than they knew. Fourthly, I demanded whence he came, their
answer was they could not tell. And fifthly, I asked whither he
went, and they replied they knew nothing of the matter, – and   50
this is all I could learn.

MRS SULLEN

But what do the people say, can't they guess?

SCRUB

Why some think he's a spy, some guess he's a mountebank,
some say one thing, some another; but for my own part, I
believe he's a Jesuit.   55

DORINDA

A Jesuit! Why a Jesuit?

SCRUB

Because he keeps his horses always ready saddled, and his
footman talks French.

MRS SULLEN

His footman!

SCRUB

Ay, he and the count's footman were gabbering French like   60
two intriguing ducks in a mill-pond, and I believe they talked
of me, for they laughed consumedly.

DORINDA

What sort of livery has the footman?

SCRUB

Livery! Lord, madam, I took him for a captain, he's so
bedizened with lace, and then he has tops to his shoes, up to   65
his mid leg, a silver-headed cane dangling at his knuckles, – he

53 *mountebank* travelling quack
56–8 *Jesuit . . . French* Catholics and the French: topical comic targets.
60 *gabbering* talking volubly, jabbering
65–6 *tops . . . leg* Archer wears high boots.

carried his hands in his pockets just so – (*Walks in the French air*) and has a fine long periwig tied up in a bag – Lord, madam, he's clear another sort of man than I.

MRS SULLEN

That may easily be – but what shall we do now, sister? 70

DORINDA

I have it. – This fellow has a world of simplicity, and some cunning, the first hides the latter by abundance. – Scrub.

SCRUB

Madam.

DORINDA

We have a great mind to know who this gentleman is, only for our satisfaction. 75

SCRUB

Yes, madam, it would be a satisfaction, no doubt.

DORINDA

You must go and get acquainted with his footman, and invite him hither to drink a bottle of your ale, because you're butler today.

SCRUB

Yes, madam, I am butler every Sunday. 80

MRS SULLEN

O brave, sister, o'my conscience, you understand the mathematics already – 'tis the best plot in the world: your mother, you know, will be gone to church, my spouse will be got to the ale-house with his scoundrels, and the house will be our own – so we drop in by accident and ask the fellow some 85 questions ourselves. In the country you know any stranger is company, and we're glad to take up with the butler in a country dance, and happy if he'll do us the favour.

SCRUB

Oh! Madam, you wrong me, I never refused your ladyship the favour in my life. 90

Enter GIPSY

---

68 *bag* a silk bag, usually black, which held the back hair of a wig
82 *mathematics* humorously implying complex matters, i.e. the intricacies of managing love affairs
90 *favour* Scrub pretends Mrs Sullen refers to sexual favours, what was referred to at this time as 'the last favour'.

GIPSY

Ladies, dinner's upon table.

DORINDA

Scrub, we'll excuse your waiting. – Go where we ordered you.

SCRUB

I shall.

Exeunt

[ACT III. SCENE ii]

Scene changes to the inn

Enter AIMWELL *and* ARCHER

ARCHER

Well, Tom, I find you're a marksman.

AIMWELL

A marksman! Who so blind could be as not discern a swan among the ravens.

ARCHER

Well, but hark'ee, Aimwell.

AIMWELL

Aimwell! Call Oroondates, Cesario, Amadis, all that romance   5
can in a lover paint, and then I'll answer. O Archer, I read her
thousands in her looks, she looked like Ceres in her harvest,
corn, wine and oil, milk and honey, gardens, groves and purling
streams played on her plenteous face.

ARCHER

Her face! Her pocket you mean; the corn, wine and oil lies there.   10
In short, she has ten thousand pound, that's the English on't.

AIMWELL

Her eyes –

---

1 *you're a marksman* Aimwell lives up to his boast, see II.ii.39.

5 *Oroondates, Cesario, Amadis* Oroondates and Cesario appear in the very lengthy seventeenth-century prose romances of La Calprenède, *Cassandra* and *Cléopâtra*. The French
hero Amadis appears in the popular romance, *Amadis de Gaul*, first printed in Spanish in
the sixteenth century. For Oroondates Cordner mentions also John Banks' play *The Rival
Kings, or, The Loves of Oroondates and Statira* (performed 1677).

7 *Ceres* Roman goddess of the harvest and fertility

ARCHER

Are demi-cannons to be sure, so I won't stand their battery.

Going

AIMWELL

Pray excuse me, my passion must have vent.

ARCHER

Passion! What a plague! D'ye think these romantic airs will do   15
our business? Were my temper as extravagant as yours, my
adventures have something more romantic by half.

AIMWELL

Your adventures!

ARCHER

Yes. The nymph that with her twice ten hundred pounds
    With brazen engine hot, and coif clear starched   20
    Can fire the guest in warming of the bed –
There's a touch of sublime Milton for you, and the subject but
an innkeeper's daughter. I can play with a girl as an angler does
with his fish; he keeps it at the end of his line, runs it up the
stream, and down the stream, till at last, he brings it to hand,   25
tickles the trout, and so whips it into his basket.

Enter BONNIFACE

BONNIFACE

Mr Martin, as the saying is – yonder's an honest fellow below,
my Lady Bountiful's butler, who begs the honour that you
would go home with him and see his cellar.

ARCHER

Do my *baisemains* to the gentleman, and tell him I will do   30
myself the honour to wait on him immediately.

Exit BONNIFACE

13 *demi-cannons* large pieces of artillery weighing six thousand pounds; a cannon weighed
seven thousand
20 *brazen engine* warming-pan
coif a close-fitting cap
22 *sublime Milton* There was a fashion for humorous verse parodying the grand style of
Milton's *Paradise Lost*. 'The most popular work of this kind was Ambrose Philips's *The
Splendid Shilling* (1701); by 1720 it had been reprinted nine times (both by itself and in
miscellanies).' (Cordner)
30 *Do my baisemains* give my compliments, respects; *baisemain* (French) a kiss on the hand

AIMWELL

What do I hear, soft Orpheus play, and fair Toftida sing?

ARCHER

Pshaw! Damn your raptures, I tell you here's a pump going to
be put into the vessel, and the ship will get into harbour, my life
on't. You say there is another lady very handsome there?   35

AIMWELL

Yes, faith.

ARCHER

I am in love with her already.

AIMWELL

Can't you give me a bill upon Cherry in the meantime?

ARCHER

No, no, friend, all her corn, wine and oil is engrossed to my
market. – And once more I warn you to keep your anchorage   40
clear of mine, for if you fall foul of me, by this light you shall
go to the bottom. – What! Make prize of my little frigate, while
I am upon the cruise for you.   *Exit*

Enter BONNIFACE

AIMWELL

Well, well, I won't. – Landlord, have you any tolerable company
in the house? I don't care for dining alone.   45

BONNIFACE

Yes, sir, there's a captain below, as the saying is, that arrived
about an hour ago.

32 *Orpheus* the musician in Greek mythology whose playing enchanted gods and men
   Toftida Katherine Tofts, the first English singer of Italian opera in England; 'the Drury
   Lane Company offered her talents as the competing attraction to the first performance of
   The Beaux' Stratagem.' (Cordner)
33–4 *here's a pump . . . harbour* Nautical metaphors: the 'pump' is Dorinda's wealth which
   will save the ship of their fortunes from sinking.
38 *bill* a note written by one person promising to pay another a certain sum, or to provide
   goods; here Cherry is the 'goods'
39 *engrossed* all bought up, monopolized, continuing Aimwell's trading metaphor
41 *fall foul of* become entangled with; originally as here a phrase used of ships' anchors and
   tackle
42 *frigate* a light, swift vessel (an obsolete sense)
43 *upon the cruise* keeping a look out (for an heiress)
   s.d. *Exit* ed. Q has *Exit* Bon. after 'cue' l. 59, duplicating Bonniface's *Exit* and omitting
   Archer's.

AIMWELL

Gentlemen of his coat are welcome everywhere; will you make
him a compliment from me, and tell him I should be glad of his
company.   50

BONNIFACE

Who shall I tell him, sir, would –

AIMWELL

[*Aside*] Ha! That stroke was well thrown in. – I'm only a
traveller like himself, and would be glad of his company, that's
all.

BONNIFACE

I obey your commands, as the saying is.   *Exit*   55

Enter ARCHER

ARCHER

S'death! I had forgot, what title will you give yourself?

AIMWELL

My brother's to be sure, he would never give me anything else,
so I'll make bold with his honour this bout – you know the rest
of your cue.

ARCHER

Ay, ay.   *Exit*   60

Enter GIBBET

GIBBET

Sir, I'm yours.

AIMWELL

'Tis more than I deserve, sir, for I don't know you.

GIBBET

(*Aside*) I don't wonder at that, sir, for you never saw me before,
I hope.

AIMWELL

And pray, sir, how came I by the honour of seeing you now?   65

GIBBET

Sir, I scorn to intrude upon a gentleman, – but my landlord –

AIMWELL

O, sir, I ask your pardon, you're the captain he told me of.

GIBBET

At your service, sir.

49

AIMWELL

What regiment, may I be so bold?

GIBBET

A marching regiment, sir, an old corps.   70

AIMWELL

(*Aside*) Very old, if your coat be regimental. – You have served
abroad, sir?

GIBBET

Yes, sir, in the plantations; 'twas my lot to be sent into the
worst service. I would have quitted it, indeed, but a man of
honour, you know – Besides, 'twas for the good of my country   75
that I should be abroad – anything for the good of one's
country – I'm a Roman for that.

AIMWELL

(*Aside*) One of the first, I'll lay my life. – You found the West
Indies very hot, sir?

GIBBET

Ay, sir, too hot for me.   80

AIMWELL

Pray, sir, han't I seen you face at Will's coffee-house?

GIBBET

Yes, sir, and at White's too.

AIMWELL

And where is your company now, captain?

GIBBET

They an't come yet.

AIMWELL

Why, d'ye expect 'em here?   85

---

70 *marching regiment* In this conversation Gibbet's answers have a double meaning for the
audience who know he is a highwayman.

73 *plantations* Convicts at this time were transported to the West Indies.

74 *worst service* referring to the notorious conditions of soldiers serving in the West Indies,
and also to those endured by the convicts

77 *Roman* 'In military parlance a soldier of foot who gave his pay to his captain to be
allowed to serve, and thus was, like an ancient Roman, serving only for the good of his
country.' (Jeffares). Gibbet served 'his country's good' by being transported.

78 *One of the first* Jeffares suggests Aimwell links Gibbet with the runaway slaves who
formed part of Rome's early population.

81 *han't* haven't; also at l. 88 and IV.ii.22.
Will's the coffee house near Covent Garden, much patronized by writers

82 *White's* another famous coffee house in St James's Street

83 *company* a subdivision of an infantry regiment headed by a captain

GIBBET

They'll be here tonight, sir.

AIMWELL

Which way do they march?

GIBBET

Across the country. – [*Aside*] The devil's in't, if I han't said
enough to encourage him to declare! But I'm afraid he's not
right; I must tack about.   90

AIMWELL

Is your company to quarter in Lichfield?

GIBBET

In this house, sir.

AIMWELL

What! All?

GIBBET

My company's but thin, ha, ha, ha, we are but three, ha,
ha, ha.   95

AIMWELL

You're merry, sir.

GIBBET

Ay, sir, you must excuse me, sir, I understand the world,
especially the art of travelling. I don't care, sir, for answering
questions directly upon the road – for I generally ride with a
charge about me.   100

AIMWELL

(*Aside*) Three or four, I believe.

GIBBET

I am credibly informed that there are highwaymen upon this
quarter, not, sir, that I could suspect a gentleman of your figure
– But truly, sir, I have got such a way of evasion upon the road,
that I don't care for speaking truth to any man.   105

AIMWELL

Your caution may be necessary. – Then I presume you're no
captain?

GIBBET

Not I, sir, captain is a good travelling name, and so I take it. It
stops a great many foolish enquiries that are generally made
about gentlemen that travel, it gives a man an air of something, 110

---

100 *charge* Gibbet means 'a sum of money', Aimwell 'shot and powder for a firearm'.

and makes the drawers obedient. – And thus far I am a
captain, and no further.

AIMWELL

And pray, sir, what is your true profession?

GIBBET

O, sir, you must excuse me – upon my word, sir, I don't think it
safe to tell you.   115

AIMWELL

Ha, ha, ha, upon my word I commend you.

Enter BONNIFACE

Well, Mr Bonniface, what's the news?

BONNIFACE

There's another gentleman below, as the saying is, that hearing
you were but two, would be glad to make the third man, if you
would give him leave.   120

AIMWELL

What is he?

BONNIFACE

A clergyman, as the saying is.

AIMWELL

A clergyman! Is he really a clergyman, or is it only his travelling
name, as my friend the captain has it?

BONNIFACE

O, sir, he's a priest and chaplain to the French officers in town.   125

AIMWELL

Is he a Frenchman?

BONNIFACE

Yes, sir, born at Brussels.

GIBBET

A Frenchman, and a priest! I won't be seen in his company, sir.
I have a value for my reputation, sir.

---

111 *drawers* of ale in a tavern, tapsters
127 *Brussels* Bonniface mistakenly believes this means Foigard is French. Brussels, previously a Spanish possession, had in the early years of the war been incorporated into the
French area of influence, but it fell to the English and allies after their victory at
Ramillies, 1706.
128 *A Frenchman . . . sir* Farquhar turns contemporary feeling against the French, in a time
of war, to comic effect, as at III.i.55–8.

AIMWELL

Nay, but captain, since we are by ourselves – can he speak   130
English, landlord?

BONNIFACE

Very well, sir, you may know him, as the saying is, to be a
foreigner by his accent, and that's all.

AIMWELL

Then he has been in England before?

BONNIFACE

Never, sir, but he's a master of languages, as the saying is. He   135
talks Latin, it does me good to hear him talk Latin.

AIMWELL

Then you understand Latin, Mr Bonniface?

BONNIFACE

Not I, sir, as the saying is, but he talks it so very fast that I'm sure
it must be good.

AIMWELL

Pray desire him to walk up.   140

BONNIFACE

Here he is, as the saying is.

Enter FOIGARD

FOIGARD

Save you, gentlemens both.

AIMWELL

A Frenchman! Sir, your most humble servant.

FOIGARD

Och, dear joy, I am your most faithful shervant, and yours
alsho.   145

GIBBET

Doctor, you talk very good English, but you have a mighty
twang of the foreigner.

FOIGARD

My English is very vel for the vords, but we foreigners you know
cannot bring our tongues about the pronunciation so soon.

---

144 *joy* a term of endearment, 'sweetheart', and here an immediate give-away since the
expression was much heard from stage Irishmen in the late seventeenth- and early
eighteenth-centuries

AIMWELL

(*Aside*) A foreigner! A downright Teague, by this light. – Were   150
you born in France, doctor?

FOIGARD

I was educated in France, but I was borned at Brussels. I am a
subject of the King of Spain, joy.

GIBBET

What King of Spain, sir, speak?

FOIGARD

Upon my shoul joy, I cannot tell you as yet.   155

AIMWELL

Nay, captain, that was too hard upon the doctor, he's a stranger.

FOIGARD

O let him alone, dear joy, I am of a nation that is not easily put
out of countenance.

AIMWELL

Come, gentlemen, I'll end the dispute. – Here, landlord, is
dinner ready?   160

BONNIFACE

Upon the table, as the saying is.

AIMWELL

Gentlemen – pray – that door –

FOIGARD

No, no, fait, the captain must lead.

AIMWELL

No, doctor, the church is our guide.

GIBBET

Ay, ay, so it is.   165

Exit foremost, they follow

---

150 *Teague* a nickname for an Irishman, compare Paddy, and also, as here, a Protestant term
of contempt for a Roman Catholic; Teague is an Irish servant in Farquhar's *The Twin-
Rivals*. Asked how he likes London, he replies: 'Fet, dear Joy, 'tis the Bravest Plaase I have
sheen in my Peregrinations, exshepting my nown brave Shitty of Carick-Vergus'
(III.ii.21–3).

154 *What King of Spain* After the death of Charles II of Spain, the War of the Spanish
Succession was fought between the French and the Grand Alliance (of Austrian, Dutch
and English forces) to determine who should succeed him: Philip of Anjou, grandson of
Louis XIV, or the Archduke Charles of Austria.

[ACT III. SCENE iii]

Scene changes to a gallery in LADY BOUNTIFUL'*s house*

Enter ARCHER *and* SCRUB *singing, and hugging one another,*
SCRUB *with a tankard in his hand,* GIPSY *listening at a distance*

SCRUB

Tall, all dall – Come, my dear boy – let's have that song once
more.

ARCHER

No, no, we shall disturb the family. But will you be sure to keep
the secret?

SCRUB

Pho! Upon my honour, as I'm a gentleman.   5

ARCHER

'Tis enough. – You must know then that my master is the Lord
Viscount Aimwell. He fought a duel t'other day in London,
wounded his man so dangerously, that he thinks fit to withdraw
till he hears whether the gentleman's wounds be mortal or not.
He never was in this part of England before, so he chose to   10
retire to this place, that's all.

GIPSY

[*Aside*] And that's enough for me.   *Exit*

SCRUB

And where were you when your master fought?

ARCHER

We never know of our masters' quarrels.

SCRUB

No! If our masters in the country here receive a challenge,   15
the first thing they do is to tell their wives; the wife tells the
servants, the servants alarm the tenants, and in half an hour you
shall have the whole county in arms.

ARCHER

To hinder two men from doing what they have no mind for. –
But if you should chance to talk now of my business?   20

SCRUB

Talk! Ay, sir, had I not learnt the knack of holding my tongue,
I had never lived so long in a great family.

ARCHER

Ay, ay, to be sure there are secrets in all families.

55

SCRUB

Secrets, ay. – But I'll say no more. – Come, sit down, we'll make
an end of our tankard. Here –   25

ARCHER

With all my heart. Who knows but you and I may come to
be better acquainted, eh? – Here's your ladies' healths; you
have three, I think, and to be sure there must be secrets among
'em.

SCRUB

Secrets! Ay, friend. I wish I had a friend –   30

ARCHER

Am not I your friend? Come, you and I will be sworn brothers.

SCRUB

Shall we?

ARCHER

From this minute. – Give me a kiss – and now, brother Scrub –

SCRUB

And now, brother Martin, I will tell you a secret that will make
your hair stand on end. – You must know that I am consumedly   35
in love.

ARCHER

That's a terrible secret, that's the truth on't.

SCRUB

That jade, Gipsy, that was with us just now in the cellar, is the
arrantest whore that ever wore a petticoat, and I'm dying for
love for her.   40

ARCHER

Ha, ha, ha. – Are you in love with her person, or her virtue,
brother Scrub?

SCRUB

I should like virtue best, because it is more durable than beauty,
for virtue holds good with some women long, and many a day
after they have lost it.   45

ARCHER

In the country, I grant ye, where no woman's virtue is lost, till a
bastard be found.

SCRUB

Ay, could I bring her to a bastard, I should have her all to

48 *bring . . . bastard* get her pregnant

myself; but I dare not put it upon that lay, for fear of being sent
for a soldier. – Pray, brother, how do you gentlemen in London   50
like that same Pressing Act?

ARCHER

Very ill, brother Scrub. – 'Tis the worst that ever was made for
us. Formerly I remember the good days, when we could dun
our masters for our wages, and if they refused to pay us, we
could have a warrant to carry 'em before a Justice; but now, if   55
we talk of eating; they have a warrant for us, to carry us before
three Justices.

SCRUB

And to be sure we go, if we talk of eating, for the Justices won't
give their own servants a bad example. Now this is my
misfortune – I dare not speak in the house, while that jade   60
Gipsy dings about like a fury. – Once I had the better end of the
staff.

ARCHER

And how comes the change now?

SCRUB

Why, the mother of all this mischief is a priest.

ARCHER

A priest!   65

SCRUB

Ay, a damned son of a whore of Babylon, that came over hither
to say grace to the French officers, and eat up our provisions. –
There's not a day goes over his head without dinner or supper
in this house.

ARCHER

How came he so familiar in the family?   70

---

49 *put it upon that lay* go in for that line of business; 'lay' (slang), line of business, adventure,
tack (*OED* quoting this line)
51 *Pressing Act* Acts introduced first in 1703 to raise men for the army; able bodied men
without employment or means of support could be conscripted on the decision of three
justices of the peace, a system Farquhar takes as a subject for critical comedy in *The
Recruiting Officer.*
53 *dun* make repeated demands for money
61–2 *better . . . staff* not the rough end of the stick
66 *whore of Babylon* the Church of Rome, according to one Protestant interpretation of
Revelation, xvii–ix

SCRUB

Because he speaks English as if he had lived here all his life, and tells lies as if he had been a traveller from his cradle.

ARCHER

And this priest, I'm afraid, has converted the affections of your Gipsy.

SCRUB

Converted! Ay, and perverted, my dear friend. – For I'm afraid   75
he has made her a whore and a papist. – But this is not all.
There's the French count and Mrs Sullen, they're in the
confederacy, and for some private ends of their own to be sure.

ARCHER

A very hopeful family yours, brother Scrub. I suppose the
maiden lady has her lover too.   80

SCRUB

Not that I know. – She's the best on 'em, that's the truth on't.
But they take care to prevent my curiosity, by giving me so
much business that I'm a perfect slave. – What d'ye think is my
place in this family?

ARCHER

Butler, I suppose.   85

SCRUB

Ah, Lord help you. – I'll tell you. – Of a Monday, I drive the
coach; of a Tuesday, I drive the plough; on Wednesday, I follow
the hounds; a Thursday, I dun the tenants; on Friday, I go to
market; on Saturday, I draw warrants; and a Sunday, I draw
beer.   90

ARCHER

Ha, ha, ha! If variety be a pleasure in life, you have enough on't,
my dear brother. – But what ladies are those?

SCRUB

Ours, ours. That upon the right hand is Mrs Sullen, and the
other is Mrs Dorinda. – Don't mind 'em, sit still, man –

Enter MRS SULLEN *and* DORINDA

72 *tells . . . cradle* Referring to the proverbial notion that travellers tell lies; compare *The Recruiting Officer*: Worthy is speaking of the braggart, Captain Brazen: 'add but the traveller's privilege of lying, and even that he abuses' (III.i.208–9).

89 *draw warrants* for his master Squire Sullen, a Justice of the Peace

93 s.p. SCRUB 1728 (*Arch.* Q)

MRS SULLEN

I have heard my brother talk of my Lord Aimwell, but they say   95
that his brother is the finer gentleman.

DORINDA

That's impossible, sister.

MRS SULLEN

He's vastly rich, but very close, they say.

DORINDA

No matter for that. If I can creep into his heart, I'll open his
breast, I warrant him. I have heard say that people may be   100
guessed at by the behaviour of their servants. I could wish we
might talk to that fellow.

MRS SULLEN

So do I, for I think he's a very pretty fellow. Come this way, I'll
throw out a lure for him presently.

> *They walk a turn towards the opposite side of the stage,*
> MRS SULLEN *drops her glove,*
> ARCHER *runs, takes it up, and gives it to her*

ARCHER

[*Aside*] Corn, wine, and oil, indeed. – But, I think, the wife has   105
the greatest plenty of flesh and blood. She should be my choice.
– Ah, a, say you so – madam – your Ladyship's glove.

MRS SULLEN

O, sir, I thank you. – [*To* DORINDA] What a handsome bow the
fellow has!

DORINDA

Bow! Why I have known several footmen come down from   110
London set up here for dancing masters, and carry off the best
fortunes in the country.

ARCHER

(*Aside*) That project, for ought I know, had been better than
ours. – Brother Scrub – why don't you introduce me?

SCRUB

Ladies, this is the strange gentleman's servant that you see at   115
church today. I understood he came from London, and so I
invited him to the cellar, that he might show me the newest
flourish in whetting my knives.

117–18 *newest . . . knives* for carving, presumably; another of Scrub's duties

DORINDA

And I hope you have made much of him?

ARCHER

O yes, madam, but the strength of your ladyship's liquor is a   120
little too potent for the constitution of your humble servant.

MRS SULLEN

What, then you don't usually drink ale?

ARCHER

No, madam, my constant drink is tea, or a little wine and water.
'Tis prescribed me by the physician for a remedy against the
spleen.   125

SCRUB

O la, O la! – A footman have the spleen.

MRS SULLEN

I thought that distemper had been only proper to people of
quality.

ARCHER

Madam, like all other fashions it wears out, and so descends to
their servants; though in a great many of us, I believe it   130
proceeds from some melancholy particles in the blood,
occasioned by the stagnation of wages.

DORINDA

[To MRS SULLEN] How affectedly the fellow talks. – How long,
pray, have you served your present master?

ARCHER

Not long. My life has been mostly spent in the service of the   135
ladies.

MRS SULLEN

And pray, which service do you like best?

ARCHER

Madam, the ladies pay best. The honour of serving them is
sufficient wages; there is a charm in their looks that delivers a
pleasure with their commands, and gives our duty the wings of   140
inclination.

MRS SULLEN

[To DORINDA] That flight was above the pitch of a livery. – And,
sir, would not you be satisfied to serve a lady again?

126 *A footman . . . spleen* John Butt, in a note on Spleen in Pope's *The Rape of the Lock*,
Canto iv, line 16, writes: 'The fashionable name for an ancient malady, the incidence of
which was jealously confined to the idle rich.' See also the note at II.i.101.

ARCHER

As a groom of the chamber, madam, but not as a footman.

MRS SULLEN

I suppose you served as footman before.   145

ARCHER

For that reason I would not serve in that post again, for my
memory is too weak for the load of messages that the ladies lay
upon their servants in London. My Lady Howd'ye, the last
mistress I served, called me up one morning, and told me,
'Martin, go to my Lady Allnight with my humble service; tell   150
her I was to wait on her Ladyship yesterday, and left word with
Mrs Rebecca that the preliminaries of the affair she knows
of are stopped till we know the concurrence of the person that
I know of, for which there are circumstances wanting which
we shall accommodate at the old place; but that in the   155
meantime there is a person about her Ladyship that, from
several hints and surmises, was accessory at a certain time to the
disappointments that naturally attend things, that to her
knowledge are of more importance.'

MRS SULLEN ⎫
DORINDA   ⎬ Ha, ha, ha! Where are you going, sir?   160

ARCHER

Why, I han't half done. – The whole Howd'ye was about half
an hour long. So I happened to misplace two syllables, and was
turned off, and rendered incapable –

DORINDA

The pleasantest fellow, sister, I ever saw. – But, friend, if your
master be married, – I presume you still serve a lady?   165

ARCHER

No, madam, I take care never to come into a married family.
The commands of the master and mistress are always so
contrary, that 'tis impossible to please both.

DORINDA

(*Aside*) There's a main point gained. – My lord is not married,
I find.   170

144 *groom of the chamber* manservant employed within the house
161 *Howd'ye* here a noun, her message; previously, l. 148, the name of lady who greets her
     friends with long messages of inquiry
163 *turned off* dismissed
     rendered represented, described as

MRS SULLEN

But, I wonder, friend, that in so many good services, you had not a better provision made for you.

ARCHER

I don't know how, madam. – I had a lieutenancy offered me three or four times, but that is not bread, madam – I live much better as I do.   175

SCRUB

Madam, he sings rarely – I was thought to do pretty well here in the country till he came, but alack a day, I'm nothing to my brother Martin.

DORINDA

Does he? Pray, sir, will you oblige us with a song?

ARCHER

Are you for passion, or humour?   180

SCRUB

O la! He has the purest ballad about a trifle –

MRS SULLEN

A trifle! Pray, sir, let's have it.

ARCHER

I'm ashamed to offer you a trifle, madam, but since you command me –

Sings to the tune of Sir Simon the King

Song of a Trifle

A trifling song you shall hear,   185
Begun with a trifle and ended:

171–2 *you had . . . you* you haven't been better provided for, i.e. by being found alternative employment

173 *lieutenancy* Farquhar had served as lieutenant, without much profit; see p. viii.

181 *O la* ed. (O le Q)

purest most excellent, finest; another colloquial use of 'pure' (*OED* IV.8); compare 'purely', III.i.38.

184 s.d. *the tune of Sir Simon the King* a popular tune first printed in Playford's *Musick's Recreation* (1652); Cordner notes that in Fielding's *Tom Jones*, it is a favourite of Squire Western (Book 4, Chapter 5). A printed broadsheet of another contemporary setting by Daniel Purcell survives in the Bodleian Library and elsewhere; see also Milhous and Hume, p. 324.

Song of a Trifle (1728, not in Q). The thirteen verses are printed from 1728 where they appear after the Epilogue. As at I.i.321, Q prints only the song's first two lines: *A trifling song . . . ended, &c.*

All trifling people draw near,
And I shall be nobly attended.

Were it not for trifles, a few,
That lately have come into play,   190
The men would want something to do
And the women want something to say.

What makes men trifle in dressing?
Because the ladies (they know)
Admire, by often possessing,   195
That eminent trifle, a beau.

When the lover his moments has trifled,
The trifle of trifles to gain,
No sooner the virgin is rifled,
But a trifle shall part 'em again.   200

What mortal man would be able
At White's half an hour to sit?
Or who could bear a tea-table
Without talking of trifles for wit?

The court is from trifles secure;   205
Gold keys are no trifles we see:
White rods are no trifles, I'm sure,
Whatever their bearer may be.

But if you will go to the place
Where trifles abundantly breed,   210
The levee will show you his Grace
Makes promises trifles indeed.

---

206 *Gold keys* the insignia of the Lord Chamberlain, among whose duties were control of
the playhouses, and licensing of plays; or, the insignia of the Groom of the Stole, the
first lord of the bedchamber in the Royal Household
207 *White rods* White staffs carried by the Lord Chamberlain as a badge of office
211 *levee* a morning assembly held by a prince or other person of distinction
his Grace Seen by some as an allusion to Farquhar's own disappointment at the hands of
the Duke of Ormond (see p. viii).

A coach with six footmen behind
I count neither trifle nor sin:
But, ye gods! How oft do we find   215
A scandalous trifle within?

A flask of champagne, people think it,
A trifle, or something as bad:
But if you'll contrive how to drink it,
You'll find it no trifle egad.   220

A parson's a trifle at sea,
A widow's a trifle in sorrow:
A peace is a trifle today;
Who knows what may happen tomorrow.

A black coat a trifle may cloak,   225
Or to hide it, the red may endeavour:
But if once the army is broke,
We shall have more trifles than ever.

The stage is a trifle they say;
The reason, pray carry along: 230
Because at every new play
The house they with trifles so throng.

But with people's malice to trifle,
And to set us all on a foot:
The author of this is a trifle,   235
And his song is a trifle to boot.

MRS SULLEN
  Very well, sir, we're obliged to you. – Something for a pair of
  gloves.   *Offering him money*

---

223 *A peace* 'a mocking allusion to the Tory desire for an end to the continental war'
    (Cordner)
225 *black coat* worn by the clergy
226 *red* red-coat, military uniform, compare I.i.7.
227 *the army is broke* i.e. disbanded; after the Peace of Ryswick (1697) when the standing
    army had been substantially reduced, controversy raged about the size of the peacetime
    standing army.

ARCHER

    I humbly beg leave to be excused. My master, madam, pays me,
    nor dare I take money from any other hand without injuring   240
    his honour, and disobeying his commands.   *Exit*

DORINDA

    This is surprising. Did you ever see so pretty a well-bred fellow?

MRS SULLEN

    The devil take him for wearing that livery.

DORINDA

    I fancy, sister, he may be some gentleman, a friend of my
    lord's, that his lordship has pitched upon for his courage,   245
    fidelity, and discretion to bear him company in this dress, and
    who, ten to one, was his second too.

MRS SULLEN

    It is so, it must be so, and it shall be so – for I like him.

DORINDA

    What! Better than the count?

MRS SULLEN

    The count happened to be the most agreeable man upon the   250
    place, and so I chose him to serve me in my design upon my
    husband. – But I should like this fellow better in a design upon
    myself.

DORINDA

    But now, sister, for an interview with this lord, and this
    gentleman. How shall we bring that about?   255

MRS SULLEN

    Patience! You country ladies give no quarter, if once you be
    entered. – Would you prevent their desires, and give the
    fellows no wishing-time. – Look ye, Dorinda, if my lord
    Aimwell loves you or deserves you, he'll find a way to see you,
    and there we must leave it. – My business comes now upon the   260
    tapis. – Have you prepared your brother?

DORINDA

    Yes, yes.

---

244 *gentleman* ed. (gentlemen Q)
247 *his second* in a duel; the audience has already heard Archer's story of the duel Aimwell is
    supposed to have fought (III.iii.7–9).
256–7 *give . . . entered* i.e. show no mercy once you are engaged in action
257 *prevent* anticipate
260–61 *upon the tapis* under discussion; literally, on the table-cloth, or *tapis* (French)

MRS SULLEN

And how did he relish it?

DORINDA

He said little, mumbled something to himself, promised to be
guided by me. But here he comes.   265

Enter SULLEN

SULLEN

What singing was that I heard just now?

MRS SULLEN

The singing in your head, my dear, you complained of it all day.

SULLEN

You're impertinent.

MRS SULLEN

I was ever so, since I became one flesh with you.

SULLEN

One flesh! Rather two carcasses joined unnaturally together.   270

MRS SULLEN

Or rather a living soul coupled to a dead body.

DORINDA

So, this is fine encouragement for me.

SULLEN

Yes, my wife shows you what you must do.

MRS SULLEN

And my husband shows you what you must suffer.

SULLEN

S'death, why can't you be silent?   275

268 *impertinent* absurd, silly, an obsolete meaning; *OED* quotes: 'the Ladies whom you visit,
     think a wise Man the most Impertinent Creature living.' Steele, *Spectator*, 148 (1704).
269 *one flesh* the words of Christ: see Matthew xix. 5–6, Mark x. 8. In the *The Double-Dealer*
     (acted 1693) Congreve plays with the phrase: 'Tho' marriage makes man and wife one
     flesh, it leaves 'em still two fools.' (II.i)
270–71 *One . . . dead body* The first of Farquhar's borrowings from Milton, see p. xxv.
     Compare Milton's 'nay, instead of being one flesh, they will be rather two carcasses
     chained unnaturally together; or, as it may happen, a living soul bound to a dead
     corpse.' (*Prose Works* II, 326, spelling modernized here and in all further quotations).
     Cordner points out that Farquhar makes Mrs Sullen reverse the conventional associ-
     ation of soul with male and body with female.

MRS SULLEN

S'death, why can't you talk?

SULLEN

Do you talk to any purpose?

MRS SULLEN

Do you think to any purpose?

SULLEN

Sister, hark ye. (*Whispers*) I shan't be home till it be late.   *Exit*

MRS SULLEN

What did he whisper to ye?   280

DORINDA

That he would go round the back way, come into the closet, and
listen as I directed him. – But let me beg you once more, dear
sister, to drop this project; for, as I told you before, instead of
awaking him to kindness, you may provoke him to a rage, and
then who knows how far his brutality may carry him?   285

MRS SULLEN

I'm provided to receive him, I warrant you. But here comes the
count, vanish!

Exit DORINDA

Enter COUNT BELLAIR

Don't you wonder, Monsieur le Count, that I was not at church
this afternoon?

COUNT

I more wonder, madam, that you go dere at all, or how you dare   290
to lift those eyes to Heaven that are guilty of so much killing.

MRS SULLEN

If Heaven, sir, has given to my eyes with the power of killing,
the virtue of making a cure, I hope the one may atone for the
other.

COUNT

O largely, madam, would your ladyship be as ready to apply the   295
remedy as to give the wound. – Consider, madam, I am doubly a
prisoner: first to the arms of your general, then to your more

287–419 The rest of the Act, from Count Bellair's entrance to the end, including Mrs
    Sullen's verses, was printed in italic in 1728 and later editions, with a note explaining
    that the scene had been 'cut out by the author, after the first night's representation.' See
    Appendix, pp. 135–6.

conquering eyes. My first chains are easy, there a ransom may
redeem me, but from your fetters I never shall get free.

MRS SULLEN

Alas, sir, why should you complain to me of your captivity, who   300
am in chains myself? You know, sir, that I am bound, nay,
must be tied up in that particular that might give you ease: I
am like you, a prisoner of war – of war indeed, – I have given
my parole of honour. Would you break yours to gain your
liberty?   305

COUNT

Most certainly I would, were I a prisoner among the Turks: dis
is your case. You're a slave, madam, slave to the worst of Turks,
a husband.

MRS SULLEN

There lies my foible, I confess. No fortifications, no courage,
conduct, nor vigilancy can pretend to defend a place, where   310
the cruelty of the governor forces the garrison to mutiny.

COUNT

And where de besieger is resolved to die before de place. – Here
will I fix, (*Kneels*) with tears, vows, and prayers assault your
heart, and never rise till you surrender; or if I must storm –
Love and St Michael – and so I begin the attack –   315

MRS SULLEN

Stand off. (*Aside*) Sure he hears me not – and I could almost

---

298 *in chains* See the note at II.i.52–3, and p. xxii.
     must ed. (most Q)
304 *parole of honour* word of honour, 'the undertaking given by a prisoner of war that he
     will not to try to escape, or that, if liberated, he will return to custody under stated
     conditions, or will refrain from taking up arms against his captors for a stated period'
     (*OED*)
306–8 *Turks ... husband* Alluding to the qualities traditionally attributed to Turks: their
     cruelty, barbarity and ill-treatment of their wives; Mary, Lady Chudleigh in her poem
     'To the Ladies' (1703) wrote of the proud husband: 'Fierce as an eastern prince he
     grows, / And all his innate rigour shows.' (*Eighteenth-Century Women Poets*, ed. Roger
     Lonsdale (Oxford, 1989), p. 3).
307 *slave* Mary Astell warns women against men's 'fine Speeches and Submissions': 'he may
     call himself her Slave a few days, but it is only in order to make her his all the rest of his
     Life' (*Reflections on Marriage, The First English Feminist*, ed. Hill, p.100).
309 *foible* weak point
310 *place* a fortress. citadel, a "strong place" (*OED*), a now obsolete meaning.
315 *St Michael* the leader of the armies in Heaven and patron saint of soldiers; the count
     invokes his help along with that of *Love*.

wish he – did not. – The fellow makes love very prettily. – But, sir, why should you put such a value on my person, when you see it despised by one that knows it so much better?

COUNT

He knows it not, though he possesses it. If he but knew the   320
value of the jewel he is master of, he would always wear it next
his heart, and sleep with it in his arms.

MRS SULLEN

But since he throws me unregarded from him –

COUNT

And one that knows your value well comes by, and takes you up,
is it not justice?   *Goes to lay hold on her*   325

Enter SULLEN *with his sword drawn*

SULLEN

Hold, villain, hold.

MRS SULLEN

(*Presenting a pistol*) Do you hold.

SULLEN

What! Murder your husband, to defend your bully.

MRS SULLEN

Bully! For shame, Mr Sullen. Bullies wear long swords, the
gentleman has none. He's a prisoner you know. – I was aware of   330
your outrage, and prepared this to receive your violence, and,
if the occasion were, to preserve myself against the force of this
other gentleman.

COUNT

O madam, your eyes be bettre firearms than your pistol. They
nevre miss.   335

SULLEN

What, court my wife to my face!

MRS SULLEN

Pray, Mr Sullen, put up, suspend your fury for a minute.

SULLEN

To give you time to invent an excuse.

329 *bully* lover, gallant, a gallant who lives by protecting prostitutes
331 *outrage* mad, passionate behaviour, fury

MRS SULLEN

I need none.

SULLEN

No, for I heard every syllable of your discourse.   340

COUNT

Ay! And begar, I tink de dialogue was vera pretty.

MRS SULLEN

Then I suppose, sir, you heard something of your own
barbarity.

SULLEN

Barbarity! Oons, what does the woman call barbarity? Do I
ever meddle with you?   345

MRS SULLEN

No.

SULLEN

As for you, sir, I shall take another time.

COUNT

Ah, begar, and so must I.

SULLEN

Look ye, madam, don't think that my anger proceeds from any
concern I have for your honour, but for my own, and if you can   350
contrive any way of being a whore without making me a
cuckold, do it and welcome.

MRS SULLEN

Sir, I thank you kindly, you would allow me the sin but rob me
of the pleasure. – No, no, I am resolved never to venture
upon the crime without the satisfaction of seeing you punished   355
for't.

SULLEN

Then will you grant me this, my dear? Let anybody else do you
the favour but that Frenchman, for I mortally hate his whole
generation.   *Exit*

COUNT

Ah, sir, that be ungrateful, for begar, I love some of yours,   360
madam.   *Approaching her*

---

341 *begar* begad, by God, a favourite exclamation of stage Frenchmen, for instance, Dr Caius
     in *The Merry Wives of Windsor*
344 *woman* ed. (women Q)
358 *the favour* a euphemism for sexual intercourse, as at III.i.90
359 *generation* family, breed, race, an obsolete sense

MRS SULLEN

No, sir.

COUNT

No, sir? – Garzoon, madam, I am not your husband.

MRS SULLEN

'Tis time to undeceive you, sir. – I believed your addresses to me
were no more than an amusement, and I hope you will think   365
the same of my complaisance, and to convince you that you
ought, you must know that I brought you hither only to make
you instrumental in setting me right with my husband, for he
was planted to listen by my appointment.

COUNT

By your appointment?   370

MRS SULLEN

Certainly.

COUNT

And so, madam, while I was telling twenty stories to part you
from your husband, begar, I was bringing you together all the
while.

MRS SULLEN

I ask your pardon, sir, but I hope this will give you a taste of the   375
virtue of the English ladies.

COUNT

Begar, madam, your virtue be vera great, but garzoon your
honeste be vera little.

Enter DORINDA

MRS SULLEN

Nay, now you're angry, sir.

COUNT

Angry! *Fair Dorinda.* (*Sings the opera tune, and addresses to*   380

---

363 *Garzoon* Another oath: God's wounds
378 *be* Kenny notes that Q has de, corrected to *be* in *Comedies* [1708]; but this copy of Q is
      already corrected.
380–82 *Fair Dorinda . . . Revenge, etc* Kenny (II, 564) identifies this as a song from the opera
      Camilla, with lyrics by Owen Swiny, revived at Drury Lane on 30 March 1706: 'Fair
      Dorinda, happy, happy, / Happy may'st thou ever be: / The stars that smile on happy
      Days. / May they all now smile on thee.' Later Dorinda sings a song of revenge, and Fifer
      suggests the Count may sing or hum bits of both songs. *Camilla* is referred to dis-
      paragingly in the Epilogue to *The Recruiting Officer* (which opened on 8 April 1706) as
      an opera which, like all operas, put many to sleep.

DORINDA) Madam, when your ladyship want a fool, send for
me. *Fair Dorinda, Revenge, etc.* *Exit*

MRS SULLEN

There goes the true humour of his nation, resentment with
good manners, and the height of anger in a song. – Well, sister,
you must be judge, for you have heard the trial. 385

DORINDA

And I bring in my brother guilty.

MRS SULLEN

But I must bear the punishment. – 'Tis hard sister.

DORINDA

I own it – but you must have patience.

MRS SULLEN

Patience! The cant of custom. – Providence sends no evil
without a remedy. Should I lie groaning under a yoke I can 390
shake off, I were accessory to my ruin, and my patience were no
better than self-murder.

DORINDA

But how can you shake off the yoke? Your divisions don't come
within the reach of the law for a divorce.

MRS SULLEN

395Law! What law can search into the remote abyss of nature, 395
what evidence can prove the unaccountable disaffections of
wedlock? Can a jury sum up the endless aversions that are
rooted in our souls, or can a bench give judgment upon
antipathies?

DORINDA

They never pretended, sister, they never meddle but in case of 400
uncleanness.

388 *own* accept
389 *Patience* Mrs Sullen's bold stand here is indebted to passages in Milton where he rejects
    enduring unhappy marriage as a trial of patience. He argues that since marital dis-
    harmony exposes us to temptation, we should, rather than stay in this perilous condi-
    tion, resist customary creeds, and sloth, and take action: 'God sends remedies, as well as
    evils' (*Prose Works* II, 277, 341).
    cant of custom the usual hypocritical advice
396–7 *disaffections of wedlock* Larson compares Milton's attack on 'the Popes' for author-
    izing 'a judicial court to toss about and divulge the unaccountable and secret reasons of
    disaffection between a man and wife, as a thing most improperly answerable to any
    such kind of trial.' (*Prose Works* II, 343).

MRS SULLEN

Uncleanness! O sister, casual violation is a transient injury,
and may possibly be repaired, but can radical hatreds be ever
reconciled? – No, no, sister, nature is the first lawgiver, and
when she has set tempers opposite, not all the golden links of   405
wedlock, nor iron manacles of law can keep 'em fast.

    Wedlock we own ordained by Heaven's decree,
    But such as Heaven ordained it first to be,
    Concurring tempers in the man and wife
    As mutual helps to draw the load of life.   410
    View all the works of providence above,
    The stars with harmony and concord move;
    View all the works of providence below,
    The fire, the water, earth and air, we know
    All in one plant agree to make it grow.   415
    Must man the chiefest work of art divine,
    Be doomed in endless discord to repine?
    No, we should injure Heaven by that surmise:
    Omnipotence is just, were man but wise.

                         [*Exeunt*]

401, 2 *uncleanness* the Biblical ground for divorce; Milton argues for its referring to the
mind as well as the body (*Prose Works* II, 244).

402 *casual violation . . . the first lawgiver* Larson compares in Milton: 'natural hatred when-
ever it arises, is a greater evil in marriage, than the accident of adultery, a greater
defrauding, a greater injustice' (*Prose Works* II, 332); 'they [men] would be juster in
their balancing between natural hatred and casual adultery; this being but a transient
injury, and soon amended . . . but the other being an unspeakable and unremitting
sorrow and offence' (*Prose Works* II, 333); 'to forbid dislike against the guiltless instinct
of nature, is not within the province of any law to reach' (*Prose Works* II, 346).

405 *golden links . . . manacles* Larson compares in Milton: 'To couple hatred therefore,
though wedlock try all her golden links, and borrow to her aid all the iron manacles and
fetters of the law, it does but seek to twist a rope of sand' (*Prose Works* II, 345).

407–19 *Wedlock . . . but wise* These lines are given rather implausibly to Betty in *Love's
Catechism.*

ACT IV. [SCENE i]

Scene continues

Enter MRS SULLEN

MRS SULLEN

Were I born an humble Turk, where women have no soul nor property, there I must sit contented. – But in England, a country whose women are its glory, must women be abused? Where women rule, must women be enslaved, nay, cheated into slavery, mocked by a promise of comfortable society into a 5 wilderness of solitude? – I dare not keep the thought about me. – O, here comes something to divert me.

Enter a COUNTRY-WOMAN

WOMAN

I come, an't please your ladyship, you're my Lady Bountiful, an't ye?

MRS SULLEN

Well, good woman, go on. 10

WOMAN

I come seventeen long mail to have a cure for my husband's sore leg.

MRS SULLEN

Your husband! What woman, cure your husband!

---

0 s.d. 1 *Scene continues* i.e. the gallery in Lady Bountiful's house
1 *an humble* See the note at II.i.18.
   Turk See the note at III.iii.306–8.
1–2 *no soul nor property* Mary Astell writes ironically: 'I know not whether or no Women are allow'd to have Souls, if they have perhaps, it is not prudent to provoke them too much . . .' (*The First Feminist*, p. 113). In England, until the Married Women's Property Act (1870), and even later in the USA, a woman's property passed into the control of her husband upon marriage.
4 *women rule* Queen Anne succeeded to the throne in 1702.
4–5 *enslaved . . . slavery* See the note at II.i.52–3.
5 *comfortable* not limited to physical ease, but also 'providing mental and spiritual support and strength' (Cordner)
8 *ladyship* Q2 (ladyships Q)
9 *an't ye* aren't you; compare l. 24 where 'an't' stands for and it

74

WOMAN

Ay, poor man, for his sore leg won't let him stir from home.

MRS SULLEN

There, I confess, you have given me a reason. Well, good   15
woman, I'll tell you what you must do. – You must lay your
husband's leg upon a table, and, with a chopping-knife, you
must lay it open as broad as you can, then you must take out the
bone, and beat the flesh soundly with a rolling-pin, then take
salt, pepper, cloves, mace and ginger, some sweet herbs, and   20
season it very well, then roll it up like brawn, and put it into
the oven for two hours.

WOMAN

Heavens reward your ladyship. I have two little babies too that
are piteous bad with the graipes, an't please ye.

MRS SULLEN

Put a little salt and pepper in their bellies, good woman.   25

Enter LADY BOUNTIFUL

I beg your ladyship's pardon for taking your business out of
your hands. I have been a-tampering here a little with one of
your patients.

LADY BOUNTIFUL

Come, good woman, don't mind this mad creature, I am the
person you want, I suppose. – What would you have, woman?   30

MRS SULLEN

She wants something for her husband's sore leg.

LADY BOUNTIFUL

What's the matter with his leg, goody?

WOMAN

It come first as one might say with a sort of dizziness in his foot,
then he had a kind of laziness in his joints, and then his leg
broke out, and then it swelled, and then it closed again, and   35
then it broke out again, and then it festered, and then it grew
better, and then it grew worse again.

MRS SULLEN

Ha, ha, ha.

21 *brawn* prepared meat of a boar or pig
32 *goody* shortened from 'good wife', used for a woman of lower rank
35 *broke out* erupted in a rash, or other skin complaint

75

LADY BOUNTIFUL

How can you be merry with the misfortunes of other people?

MRS SULLEN

Because my own make me sad, madam. 40

LADY BOUNTIFUL

The worst reason in the world, daughter. Your own misfortunes should teach you to pity others.

MRS SULLEN

But the woman's misfortunes and mine are nothing alike. Her husband is sick, and mine, alas, is in health.

LADY BOUNTIFUL

What, would you wish your husband sick? 45

MRS SULLEN

Not of a sore leg, of all things.

LADY BOUNTIFUL

Well, good woman, go to the pantry, get your bellyful of victuals, then I'll give you a receipt of diet-drink for your husband. – But d'ye hear, goody, you must not let your husband move too much. 50

WOMAN

No, no, madam, the poor man's inclinable enough to lie still.

Exit

LADY BOUNTIFUL

Well, daughter Sullen, though you laugh, I have done miracles about the country here with my receipts.

MRS SULLEN

Miracles, indeed, if they have cured anybody, but, I believe, madam, the patient's faith goes further toward the miracle than 55 your prescription.

LADY BOUNTIFUL

Fancy helps in some cases, but there's your husband who has as little fancy as anybody, I brought him from death's door.

MRS SULLEN

I suppose, madam, you made him drink plentifully of ass's milk. 60

---

48 *receipt* recipe

    diet-drink See the note at II.i.30.

57 *Fancy* Imagination

59–60 *ass's milk* prescribed in the eighteenth century for a number of complaints; here, with a glance at Sullen's stupidity

Enter DORINDA, *runs to* MRS SULLEN

DORINDA
News, dear sister, news, news.

Enter ARCHER *running*

ARCHER
Where, where is my Lady Bountiful? – Pray, which is the old lady of you three?

LADY BOUNTIFUL
I am.

ARCHER
O, madam, the fame of your ladyship's charity, goodness,   65
benevolence, skill and ability have drawn me hither to implore
your ladyship's help in behalf of my unfortunate master, who is
this moment breathing his last.

LADY BOUNTIFUL
Your master! Where is he?

ARCHER
At your gate, madam, drawn by the appearance of your   70
handsome house to view it nearer, and walking up the avenue
within five paces of the courtyard, he was taken ill of a sudden
with a sort of I know not what, but down he fell, and there he
lies.

LADY BOUNTIFUL
Here, Scrub, Gipsy, all run, get my easy chair down stairs, put   75
the gentleman in it, and bring him in, quickly, quickly.

ARCHER
Heaven will reward your ladyship for this charitable act.

LADY BOUNTIFUL
Is your master used to these fits?

ARCHER
O yes, madam, frequently. – I have known him have five or six
of a night.   80

LADY BOUNTIFUL
What's his name?

---

78 *Is your . . . fits?* i.e. Does your master have these fits often?

ARCHER

Lord, madam, he's a-dying, a minute's care or neglect may save or destroy his life.

LADY BOUNTIFUL

Ah, poor gentleman! Come, friend, show me the way, I'll see him brought in myself. *Exit with* ARCHER 85

DORINDA

O sister, my heart flutters about strangely, I can hardly forbear running to his assistance.

MRS SULLEN

And I'll lay my life, he deserves your assistance more than he wants it. Did not I tell you that my lord would find a way to come at you? Love's his distemper, and you must be the 90 physician. Put on all your charms, summon all your fire into your eyes, plant the whole artillery of your looks against his breast, and down with him.

DORINDA

O sister, I'm but a young gunner. I shall be afraid to shoot for fear the piece should recoil and hurt myself. 95

MRS SULLEN

Never fear, you shall see me shoot before you, if you will.

DORINDA

No, no, dear sister, you have missed your mark so unfortunately that I shan't care for being instructed by you.

Enter AIMWELL *in a chair, carried by* ARCHER *and* SCRUB,
LADY BOUNTIFUL, GIPSY; AIMWELL *counterfeiting a swoon*

LADY BOUNTIFUL

Here, here, let's see the hartshorn drops. – Gipsy, a glass of 100fair water, his fit's very strong. – Bless me, how his hands are 100 clenched.

ARCHER

For shame, ladies, what d'ye do? Why don't you help us? (*To* DORINDA) Pray, madam, take his hand and open it if you can, whilst I hold his head. DORINDA *takes his hand*

89 *wants* needs
95 *piece* gun
99 *hartshorn drops* smelling-salts, carbonate of ammonia, originally prepared from harts' antlers
100 *fair water* clean, pure water

DORINDA

Poor gentleman. – Oh – he has got my hand within his, and   105
squeezes it unmercifully –

LADY BOUNTIFUL

'Tis the violence of his convulsion, child.

ARCHER

O, madam, he's perfectly possessed in these cases – he'll bite if
you don't have a care.

DORINDA

Oh, my hand, my hand.   110

LADY BOUNTIFUL

What's the matter with the foolish girl? I have got this hand
open, you see, with a great deal of ease.

ARCHER

Ay, but, madam, your daughter's hand is somewhat warmer
than your ladyship's, and the heat of it draws the force of the
spirits that way.   115

MRS SULLEN

I find, friend, you're very learned in these sorts of fits.

ARCHER

'Tis no wonder, madam, for I'm often troubled with them
myself; I find myself extremely ill at this minute.

Looking hard at MRS SULLEN

MRS SULLEN

(*Aside*) I fancy I could find a way to cure you.

LADY BOUNTIFUL

His fit holds him very long.   120

ARCHER

Longer than usual, madam. – Pray, young lady, open his breast,
and give him air.

LADY BOUNTIFUL

Where did his illness take him first, pray?

ARCHER

Today at church, madam.

---

108 *possessed* in the power of demons or spirits who might make him violent: 'he'll bite'
113 *hand . . . warmer* Farquhar makes medical conditions metaphors for sexual attraction:
Dorinda's youthful warmth attracts the force of Aimwell's spirits.
115 *spirits* On one level, as Cordner suggests, Archer refers to the vital spirits circulating in
Aimwell's body, but he also implies Aimwell is possessed by his desire for Dorinda.

LADY BOUNTIFUL

   In what manner was he taken?   125

ARCHER

   Very strangely, my lady. He was of a sudden touched with
something in his eyes, which at the first he only felt, but could
not tell whether 'twas pain or pleasure.

LADY BOUNTIFUL

   Wind, nothing but wind.

ARCHER

   By soft degrees it grew and mounted to his brain. There his   130
fancy caught it, there formed it so beautiful, and dressed it up in
such gay pleasing colours, that his transported appetite seized
the fair idea, and straight conveyed it to his heart. That
hospitable seat of life sent its sanguine spirits forth to meet,
and opened all its sluicy gates to take the stranger in.   135

LADY BOUNTIFUL

   Your master should never go without a bottle to smell to. –
Oh, he recovers! – The lavender water – some feathers to burn
under his nose – Hungary-water to rub his temples. – O, he
comes to himself. Hem a little, sir, hem. – Gipsy, bring the
cordial-water.   140

                      AIMWELL *seems to awake in amaze*

DORINDA

   How d'ye, sir?

AIMWELL

   Where am I?   *Rising*

      Sure I have passed the gulf of silent death,
      And now I land on the Elysian shore –

134 *sanguine spirits* vital spirits, spirits of blood, one of the body's four essential humours
    which, in traditional medicine, were believed to govern health and mood (the others
    being phlegm, choler and melancholy)
136 *bottle to smell* smelling-salts
137 *feathers to burn* The smell of burnt feathers was believed to act as a stimulant in fainting
    fits.
138 *Hungary-water* a stimulant made with distilled wine and rosemary flowers, named after
    the Queen of Hungary, who was said to have been given the recipe by a hermit
140 *cordial-water* preparation believed to stimulate the heart
144 *Elysian shore* the boundary of the mythical Elysian Fields where the blessed enjoyed
    immortality in idyllic surroundings

Behold the goddess of those happy plains,   145
Fair Proserpine – let me adore thy bright divinity.
                    Kneels to DORINDA *and kisses her hand*

MRS SULLEN
So, so, so, I knew where the fit would end.
AIMWELL
Eurydice perhaps –
How could thy Orpheus keep his word,
And not look back upon thee;   150
No treasure but thyself could sure have bribed him
To look one minute off thee.
LADY BOUNTIFUL
Delirious, poor gentleman.
ARCHER
Very delirious, madam, very delirious.
AIMWELL
Martin's voice, I think.   155
ARCHER
Yes, my lord. – How does your lordship?
LADY BOUNTIFUL
Lord! Did you mind that, girls?
AIMWELL
Where am I?
ARCHER
In very good hands, sir. – You were taken just now with one of
your old fits under the trees just by this good lady's house. Her   160
ladyship had you taken in, and has miraculously brought you to
yourself, as you see.
AIMWELL
I am so confounded with shame, madam, that I can now
only beg pardon – and refer my acknowledgements for your
ladyship's care, till an opportunity offers of making some   165
amends. – I dare be no longer troublesome. – Martin, give two
guineas to the servants.   *Going*

---

146 *Proserpine* the daughter of Jupiter and Ceres, forcibly taken by Pluto, the king of the
  underworld, to reign with him below
148–52 *Eurydice ... thee* On the death of his wife Eurydice, Orpheus descended to the
  underworld, and, by his powerful music, won from Pluto the right to lead her back to
  earth, provided he did not look back at her until he reached the upper earth. He did
  turn to see if she followed him, and lost her forever.

DORINDA

Sir, you may catch cold by going so soon into the air; you don't look, sir, as if you were perfectly recovered.

Here ARCHER *talks to* LADY BOUNTIFUL *in dumb show*

AIMWELL

That I shall never be, madam. My present illness is so rooted   170
that I must expect to carry it to my grave.

MRS SULLEN

Don't despair, sir, I have known several in your distemper shake it off, with a fortnight's physic.

LADY BOUNTIFUL

Come, sir, your servant has been telling me that you are apt to relapse if you go into the air. – Your good manners shan't get   175
the better of ours. – You shall sit down again, sir. – Come, sir, we don't mind ceremonies in the country. – Here, sir, my service t'ye. – You shall taste my water; 'tis a cordial, I can assure you, and of my own making – drink it off, sir. (AIMWELL *drinks*) And how d'ye find yourself now, sir?   180

AIMWELL

Somewhat better – though very faint still.

LADY BOUNTIFUL

Ay, ay, people are always faint after these fits. – Come girls, you shall show the gentleman the house, 'tis but an old family building, sir, but you had better walk about and cool by degrees than venture immediately into the air. – You'll find   185
some tolerable pictures. – Dorinda, show the gentleman the way. I must go to the poor woman below.   *Exit*

DORINDA

This way, sir.

AIMWELL

Ladies, shall I beg leave for my servant to wait on you, for he understands pictures very well?   190

MRS SULLEN

Sir, we understand originals, as well as he does pictures, so he may come along.

184–5 *cool by degrees* Aimwell's 'distemper' (l. 172) is referred to according to traditional medicine; he must regain a healthy balance. Archer and Mrs Sullen enjoy making a series of double entendres, implying Aimwell's sickness is sexual desire.

191 *originals* playing on two senses, original paintings and 'eccentric, unique characters' (Trussler)

Exeunt DORINDA, MRS SULLEN, AIMWELL, ARCHER,
AIMWELL *leads* DORINDA

Enter FOIGARD *and* SCRUB, *meeting*

FOIGARD
Save you, master Scrub.
SCRUB
Sir, I won't be saved your way. – I hate a priest, I abhor the
French, and I defy the devil. – Sir, I'm a bold Briton, and will   195
spill the last drop of my blood to keep out popery and slavery.
FOIGARD
Master Scrub, you would put me down in politics, and so I
would be speaking with Mrs Shipsey.
SCRUB
Good Mr Priest, you can't speak with her, she's sick, sir, she's
gone abroad, sir, she's – dead two months ago, sir.   200

Enter GIPSY

GIPSY
How now, impudence! How dare you talk so saucily to the
doctor? Pray, sir, don't take it ill, for the common people of
England are not so civil to strangers, as –
SCRUB
You lie, you lie. – 'Tis the common people that are civilest to
strangers.   205
GIPSY
Sirrah, I have a good mind to – Get you out, I say.
SCRUB
I won't.
GIPSY
You won't, sauce-box. – Pray, doctor, what is the captain's name
that came to your inn last night?
SCRUB
The captain! Ah, the devil, there she hampers me again. – The   210
captain has me on one side, and the priest on t'other, – so

194–6 *Sir . . . slavery* topical patriotic defiance of the Catholic French with comic effect;
 compare ll. 312–13 below.
197 *put me down* have the better of me

between the gown and the sword, I have a fine time on't. – But
Cedunt arma togae.   *Going*

GIPSY

What, sirrah, won't you march?

SCRUB

No, my dear, I won't march – but I'll walk – [*Aside*] and I'll   215
make bold to listen a little too.

Goes behind the side-scene, and listens

GIPSY

Indeed, doctor, the count has been barbarously treated, that's
the truth on't.

FOIGARD

Ah, Mrs Gipsy, upon my shoul, now, gra, his complainings
would mollify the marrow in your bones, and move the bowels   220
of your commiseration. He veeps, and he dances, and he fistles,
and he swears, and he laughs, and he stamps, and he sings. In
conclusion, joy, he's afflicted, *à la francais*, and a stranger would
not know whider to cry, or to laugh with him.

GIPSY

What would you have me do, doctor?   225

FOIGARD

Noting, joy, but only hide the count in Mrs Sullen's closet when
it is dark.

GIPSY

Nothing! Is that nothing? It would be both a sin and a shame,
doctor.

FOIGARD

Here is twenty louis d'ors, joy, for your shame; and I will give   230
you an absolution for the shin.

GIPSY

But won't that money look like a bribe?

FOIGARD

Dat is according as you shall tauk it. – If you receive the money

---

213 *Cedunt arma togae* arms yield to the gown, a well-known phrase from Cicero (*De
    Officiis* 1.22)
216 s.d. *side-scene* one of the wings, i.e. narrow pieces of scenery, parallel to the stage front
    on either stage of the stage
219 *gra* a ghráidh: Irish for love, dear, 'An exclamation ascribed to Irishmen' (*OED*)
230 *louis d'ors* gold coins issued first by Louis XIII

beforehand, 'twill be *logicé* a bribe, but if you stay till
afterwards, 'twill be only a gratification.   235

GIPSY

Well, doctor, I'll take it *logicé*. – But what must I do with my
conscience, sir?

FOIGARD

Leave dat wid me, joy. I am your priest, gra, and your
conscience is under my hands.

GIPSY

But should I put the count into the closet?   240

FOIGARD

Vel, is dere any shin for a man's being in a closhet? One may go
to prayers in a closhet.

GIPSY

But if the lady should come into her chamber, and go to bed?

FOIGARD

Vel, is dere any shin in going to bed, joy?

GIPSY

Ay, but if the parties should meet, doctor?   245

FOIGARD

Vel den – the parties must be responsible. – Do you be after
putting the count in the closet, and leave the shins with
themselves. – I will come with the count to instruct you in your
chamber.

GIPSY

Well, doctor, your religion is so pure. – Methinks I'm so easy   250
after an absolution, and can sin afresh with so much security,
that I'm resolved to die a martyr to't. – Here's the key of the
garden door. Come in the back way when 'tis late, – I 'll be ready
to receive you; but don't so much as whisper, only take hold of
my hand, I'll lead you, and do you lead the count, and follow   255
me.

Exeunt

Enter SCRUB

234 *logicé* according to logic
235 *gratification* gratuity
250–52 *Methinks . . . to't.* The bribing of Gipsy offers Farquhar the chance to incorporate
some familiar Protestant caricatures of Catholic doctrine.

SCRUB

What witchcraft now have these two imps of the devil been a-hatching here? – There's twenty louis d'ors, I heard that, and saw the purse. But I must give room to my betters.

Enter AIMWELL *leading* DORINDA, *and making love in dumb show,*
MRS SULLEN *and* ARCHER

MRS SULLEN

(*To* ARCHER) Pray, sir, how d'ye like that piece? 260

ARCHER

O, 'tis Leda. – You find, madam, how Jupiter comes disguised to make love –

MRS SULLEN

But what think you there of Alexander's battles?

ARCHER

We want only a Le Brun, madam, to draw greater battles, and a greater general of our own. – The Danube, madam, would 265 make a greater figure in a picture than the Granicus, and we have our Ramillies to match their Arbela.

MRS SULLEN

Pray, sir, what head is that in the corner there?

ARCHER

O, madam, 'tis poor Ovid in his exile.

260–300 For the relation between this dialogue and seventeenth- and eighteenth-century writing about painting, and especially the device of the picture gallery in poems and plays, see Jean H. Hagstrum's study of 'literary pictorialism', *The Sister Arts* (1958, rptd. Chicago 1974), pp. 102–3, 114–17, 238–9. The scene in Sheridan's *The School for Scandal* (1777) where Charles Surface sells off the family pictures (Act IV.i) is perhaps a late instance.

261 *Leda* The rape of Leda by Jupiter in the form of a swan was a favourite subject for painters.

263 *Alexander's battles* Alexander the Great of Macedon (356–323 BC) renowned for his military genius and huge conquests; Alexander, in Farquhar's day, was a figure familiar from his appearance in the popular play by Nathaniel Lee, *The Rival Queens* (1677, and often revived).

264 *Le Brun* French painter, 1619–90, court painter to Louis XIV, famous for his huge battle scenes, including four depicting Alexander's battles

265 *greater general* Archer compares Marlborough's victories over the French in 1704 at Blenheim, on the river Danube, and at Ramillies (1706) with Alexander's victories over the Persians by the river Granicus (334 BC), and over the Persian king, Darius at Arbela in Assyria (331 BC).

269 *Ovid* the Roman poet, banished by the emperor Augustus for some offence (possibly his *Art of Love*) to Tomi on the Black Sea

MRS SULLEN

    What was he banished for?   270

ARCHER

    His ambitious love, madam. (*Bowing*) His misfortune touches
    me.

MRS SULLEN

    Was he successful in his amours?

ARCHER

    There he has left us in the dark. – He was too much a gentleman
    to tell.   275

MRS SULLEN

    If he were secret, I pity him.

ARCHER

    And if he were successful, I envy him.

MRS SULLEN

    How d'ye like that Venus over the chimney?

ARCHER

    Venus! I protest, madam, I took it for your picture; but now I
    look again, 'tis not handsome enough.   280

MRS SULLEN

    Oh, what a charm is flattery! If you would see my picture, there
    it is, over that cabinet. – How d'ye like it?

ARCHER

    I must admire anything, madam, that has the least resemblance
    of you. – But, methinks, madam – (*He looks at the picture and*
    MRS SULLEN *three or four times, by turns*) Pray, madam, who   285
    drew it?

MRS SULLEN

    A famous hand, sir.

                                  Here AIMWELL *and* DORINDA *go off*

ARCHER

    A famous hand, madam. – Your eyes, indeed, are featured there,
    but where's the sparkling moisture, shining fluid in which they
    swim? The picture indeed has your dimples, but where's the   290
    swarm of killing Cupids that should ambush there? The lips too
    are figured out, but where's the carnation dew, the pouting
    ripeness that tempts the taste in the original?

276 *If he were secret* If he did not reveal the lady's name
278 *Venus* goddess of Love

MRS SULLEN

[*Aside*] Had it been my lot to have matched with such a man!

ARCHER

Your breasts too, presumptuous man! What, paint Heaven!   295
Apropos, madam, in the very next picture is Salmoneus, that
was struck dead with lightning, for offering to imitate Jove's
thunder. I hope you served the painter so, madam?

MRS SULLEN

Had my eyes the power of thunder, they should employ their
lightning better.   300

ARCHER

There's the finest bed in that room, madam. I suppose 'tis your
ladyship's bed chamber?

MRS SULLEN

And what then, sir?

ARCHER

I think the quilt is the richest that ever I saw. – I can't, at this
distance, madam, distinguish the figures of the embroidery.   305
Will you give me leave, madam –

MRS SULLEN

[*Aside*] The devil take his impudence. – Sure if I gave him an
opportunity, he durst not offer it. – I have a great mind to try. –
(*Going; returns*) S'death, what am I doing? – And alone too! –
Sister, sister!   *Runs out*   310

ARCHER

I'll follow her close.
    For where a Frenchman durst attempt to storm,
    A Briton sure may well the work perform.   *Going*

Enter SCRUB

SCRUB

Martin, brother Martin.

ARCHER

O, brother Scrub, I beg your pardon, I was not a-going. Here's a   315
guinea my master ordered you.

---

296 *Salmoneus* According to the legend, he offended Zeus by making a noise like thunder
    and throwing firebrands in imitation of thunderbolts, and for this was tortured in the
    underworld.

SCRUB

A guinea, hi, hi, hi, a guinea! Eh – by this light it is a guinea. But
I suppose you expect one and twenty shillings in change.

ARCHER

Not at all. I have another for Gipsy.

SCRUB

A guinea for her! Faggot and fire for the witch. – Sir, give me   320
that guinea, and I'll discover a plot.

ARCHER

A plot!

SCRUB

Ay, sir, a plot, and a horrid plot. – First, it must be a plot because
there's a woman in't; secondly, it must be a plot because there's
priest in't; thirdly, it must be a plot because there's French   325
gold in't; and fourthly, it must be a plot because I don't know
what to make on't.

ARCHER

Nor anybody else, I'm afraid, brother Scrub.

SCRUB

Truly I'm afraid so too, for where there's a priest and a woman
there's always a mystery and a riddle. – This I know, that here   330
has been the doctor with a temptation in one hand, and an
absolution in the other; and Gipsy has sold herself to the devil.
I saw the price paid down, mine eyes shall take their oath on't.

ARCHER

And is all this bustle about Gipsy?

SCRUB

That's not all. I could hear but a word here and there, but I   335
remember, they mentioned a count, a closet, and a back door,
and a key.

ARCHER

The count! Did you hear nothing of Mrs Sullen?

SCRUB

I did hear some word that sounded that way, but whether it was
Sullen or Dorinda I could not distinguish.   340

---

321 *plot* Scrub's mention of French gold and a priest recalls the frenzy of anti-Catholic
feeling aroused in 1678 by rumours of a 'damnable and hellish plot contrived and
carried on by the Popish recusants for the assassination and murdering the King,
subverting government and rooting out the Protestant religion' (Lord Shaftesbury,
quoted in Claire Tomalin, *Samuel Pepys: The Unequalled Self*, p. 314).

ARCHER

You have told this matter to nobody, brother?

SCRUB

Told! No, sir, I thank you for that. I'm resolved never to speak one word, *pro* or *con*, till we have a peace.

ARCHER

You're i'th'right, brother Scrub. Here's a treaty afoot between the count and the lady. – The priest and the chamber maid are 345 the plenipotentiaries. – It shall go hard but I find a way to be included in the treaty. – Where's the doctor now?

SCRUB

He and Gipsy are this moment devouring my lady's marmalade in the closet.

AIMWELL

(*From without*) Martin, Martin. 350

ARCHER

I come, sir, I come.

SCRUB

But you forget the other guinea, brother Martin.

ARCHER

Here, I give it with all my heart.

SCRUB

And I take it with all my soul.

[*Exit* ARCHER]

Ecod, I'll spoil your plotting, Mrs Gipsy. And if you should set 355 the captain upon me, these two guineas will buy me off. *Exit*

Enter MRS SULLEN *and* DORINDA, *meeting*

MRS SULLEN

Well, sister.

DORINDA

Well, sister.

---

343 *pro or con* for or against (Latin), another instance of Scrub's 'pretensions to gentility' (Cordner); compare l. 213.
346 *plenipotentiaries* those invested with full power to act, for instance by a sovereign in negociating a treaty; this and cognate words are additions to diplomatic language in the second half of the seventeenth century.
354 s.d. *Exit* ARCHER ed. (*Exeunt severally* Q)

MRS SULLEN

What's become of my lord?

DORINDA

What's become of his servant?   360

MRS SULLEN

Servant! He's a prettier fellow, and a finer gentleman by fifty
degrees than his master.

DORINDA

O'my conscience, I fancy you could beg that fellow at the
gallows-foot.

MRS SULLEN

O'my conscience, I could, provided I could put a friend of   365
yours in his room.

DORINDA

You desired me, sister, to leave you when you transgressed the
bounds of honour.

MRS SULLEN

Thou dear censorious country girl – what dost mean? You can't
think of the man without the bedfellow, I find.   370

DORINDA

I don't find anything unnatural in that thought; while the mind
is conversant with flesh and blood, it must conform to the
humours of the company.

MRS SULLEN

How a little love and good company improves a woman. Why,
child, you begin to live. – You never spoke before.   375

DORINDA

Because I was never spoke to. – My lord has told me that I have
more wit and beauty than any of my sex, and truly, I begin to
think the man is sincere.

MRS SULLEN

You are in the right, Dorinda, pride is the life of a woman, and
flattery is our daily bread, and she's a fool that won't believe a   380
man there, as much as she that believes him in anything else. –
But I'll lay you a guinea that I had finer things said to me than
you had.

363–4 *beg . . . gallows-foot* Dorinda accuses Mrs Sullen of being so infatuated that if Archer
were on the gallows she would beg for his life. A condemned man might be spared if a
woman asked for his pardon and was prepared to marry him.
365–6 *put a friend . . . room* i.e. have Sullen hanged instead

DORINDA

Done. – What did your fellow say to ye?

MRS SULLEN

My fellow took the picture of Venus for mine.   385

DORINDA

But my lover took me for Venus herself.

MRS SULLEN

Common cant! Had my spark called me a Venus directly, I
should have believed him a footman in good earnest.

DORINDA

But my lover was upon his knees to me.

MRS SULLEN

And mine was upon his tiptoes to me.   390

DORINDA

Mine vowed to die for me.

MRS SULLEN

Mine swore to die with me.

DORINDA

Mine spoke the softest moving things.

MRS SULLEN

Mine had his moving things too.

DORINDA

Mine kissed my hand ten thousand times.   395

MRS SULLEN

Mine has all that pleasure to come.

DORINDA

Mine offered marriage.

MRS SULLEN

O Lard! D'ye call that a moving thing?

DORINDA

The sharpest arrow in his quiver, my dear sister. – Why, my
ten thousand pounds may lie brooding here this seven years,   400
and hatch nothing at last but some ill-natured clown like
yours. – Whereas, if I marry my lord Aimwell, there will be title,

---

387 *spark* 'A lively, splendid, showy gay man. It is commonly used in contempt' (Johnson's
Dictionary). Mrs Sullen is admiring rather than contemptuous.

391 *die* Mistress of the sexual innuendo, Mrs Sullen uses 'die' to mean 'have an orgasm', a
sense common in the seventeenth- and eighteenth-centuries.

398 *Lard* an obsolete form of Lord

401 *clown* a country-man, and hence someone rude, unrefined

place and precedence, the park, the play, and the drawing-room, splendour, equipage, noise and flambeaux. – 'Hey, my lady Aimwell's servants there – lights, lights to the stairs – my lady 405 Aimwell's coach put forward – stand by, make room for her ladyship.' Are not these things moving? – What, melancholy of a sudden?

MRS SULLEN

Happy, happy sister! Your angel has been watchful for your happiness, whilst mine has slept regardless of his charge. – Long 410 smiling years of circling joys for you, but not one hour for me!   *Weeps*

DORINDA

Come, my dear, we'll talk of something else.

MRS SULLEN

O, Dorinda, I own myself a woman, full of my sex, a gentle, generous soul, – easy and yielding to soft desires, a spacious 415 heart, where love and all his train might lodge. And must the fair apartment of my breast be made a stable for a brute to lie in?

DORINDA

Meaning your husband, I suppose?

MRS SULLEN

Husband! No – even husband is too soft a name for him. – But 420 come, I expect my brother here tonight or tomorrow. He was abroad when my father married me; perhaps he'll find a way to make me easy.

DORINDA

Will you promise not to make yourself easy in the meantime with my lord's friend?   425

MRS SULLEN

You mistake me, sister. – It happens with us, as among the men, the greatest talkers are the greatest cowards, and there's a reason for't. Those spirits evaporate in prattle which might do more mischief if they took another course. – Though to confess the truth, I do love that fellow, – and if I met him dressed as he 430 should be, and I undressed as I should be – look ye, sister, I have no supernatural gifts, – I can't swear I could resist the temptation, – though I can safely promise to avoid it; and that's as much as the best of us can do.

                                        Exit MRS SULLEN *and* DORINDA

404 *flambeaux* torches

[ACT IV. SCENE ii]

[*Scene: the inn*]

Enter AIMWELL *and* ARCHER *laughing*

ARCHER

And the awkward kindness of the good motherly old
gentlewoman –

AIMWELL

And the coming easiness of the young one. – S'death, 'tis pity to
deceive her.

ARCHER

Nay, if you adhere to those principles, stop where you are.   5

AIMWELL

I can't stop, for I love her to distraction.

ARCHER

S'death, if you love her a hair's breadth beyond discretion, you
must go no further.

AIMWELL

Well, well, anything to deliver us from sauntering away our
idle evenings at White's, Tom's or Will's, and be stinted to   10
bear looking at our old acquaintance, the cards, because our
impotent pockets can't afford us a guinea for the mercenary
drabs.

ARCHER

Or be obliged to some purse-proud coxcomb for a scandalous
bottle, where we must not pretend to our share of the discourse,   15
because we can't pay our club o'th' reckoning. – Damn it, I had
rather spunge upon Morris, and sup upon a dish of bohea
scored behind the door.

---

10 *Tom's* a coffeehouse in Russell Street named after the owner, Thomas West
10–11 *be . . . at* be restricted to endure looking at
12 *impotent pockets* i.e. their lack of money means they cannot pay prostitutes
13 *drabs* prostitutes
14 *coxcomb* foolish, conceited fellow
16 *club o'th'reckoning* share of the bill
17 *Morris* owner of a coffeehouse
   bohea fine black tea

AIMWELL

And there expose our want of sense by talking criticisms, as we
should our want of money by railing at the government.   20

ARCHER

Or be obliged to sneak into the side-box, and between both
houses steal two acts of a play, and because we han't money to
see the other three, we come away discontented, and damn the
whole five.

AIMWELL

And ten thousand such rascally tricks, – had we outlived our   25
fortunes among our acquaintance. But now –

ARCHER

Ay, now is the time to prevent all this. – Strike while the iron is
hot. – This priest is the luckiest part of our adventure. – He shall
marry you and pimp for me.

AIMWELL

But I should not like a woman that can be so fond of a   30
Frenchman.

ARCHER

Alas, sir, necessity has no law. The lady may be in distress.
Perhaps she has a confounded husband, and her revenge may
carry her further than her love. – Egad, I have so good an
opinion of her, and of myself, that I begin to fancy strange   35
things, and we must say this for the honour of our women, and
indeed of ourselves, that they do stick to their men, as they
do to their Magna Carta. – If the plot lies as I suspect, – I must
put on the gentleman. – But here comes the doctor. – I shall be
ready.   *Exit*   40

Enter FOIGARD

21–2 *sneak . . . play* 'Payment for boxes was not collected until after the second act, until
which time one could leave without paying' (Fifer).
   both houses the Drury Lane Theatre, and the Queen's Theatre in the Haymarket; they
   steal an act at each.
25 *had we* if we had
29 *marry you* Marriages conducted by Catholic priests were legally binding, but it was illegal
   for priests to conduct them: those who did so were liable to a fine of £100.
37–8 *as they . . . Carta* as the men do to their legally enshrined rights (or, but less likely, as
   they (the women) do

FOIGARD

Sauve you, noble friend.

AIMWELL

O sir, your servant. Pray, doctor, may I crave your name?

FOIGARD

Fat naam is upon me? My naam is Foigard, joy.

AIMWELL

Foigard, a very good name for a clergyman. Pray, doctor
Foigard, were you ever in Ireland?   45

FOIGARD

Ireland! No, joy. – Fat sort of plaace is dat saam Ireland? Dey say
de people are catched dere when dey are young.

AIMWELL

And some of 'em when they're old. – As, for example: (*Takes*
FOIGARD *by the shoulder*) sir, I arrest you as a traitor against
the Government. You're a subject of England, and this morning   50
showed me a commission, by which you served as chaplain in
the French army. This is death by our law, and your reverence
must hang for't.

FOIGARD

Upon my shoul, noble friend, dis is strange news you tell me.
Fader Foigard a subject of England, de son of a burgomaster of   55
Brussels, a subject of England! Ubooboo –

AIMWELL

The son of a bog-trotter in Ireland. Sir, your tongue will
condemn you before any bench in the kingdom.

FOIGARD

And is my tongue all your evidench, joy?

AIMWELL

That's enough.   60

FOIGARD

No, no, joy, for I vill never spake English no more.

---

44 *good name for a clergyman* shield of faith (French)
47 *catched dere* caught there, but otherwise obscure; Myers suggests: 'probably in the sense
    of tricked or deceived – by priests like himself'.
56 *Brussels* See the note at III.ii.127.
    Ubooboo also appears in Farquhar's *The Twin Rivals* as an Irishman's exclamation (V.iii.)
57 *bog-trotter* 'applied to the wild Irish in the seventeenth century; continued in the eight-
    eenth as a nickname for Irishmen' (*OED*)

AIMWELL

Sir, I have other evidence. – Here, Martin, you know this fellow.

Enter ARCHER

ARCHER

(*In a brogue*) Saave you, my dear cussen, how does your health?

FOIGARD

(*Aside*) Ah! Upon my shoul dere is my countryman, and his 65
brogue will hang mine. – *Mynheer, ick wet neat watt hey zacht, ick universton ewe neat, sacramant.*

AIMWELL

Altering your language won't do, sir, this fellow knows your person, and will swear to your face.

FOIGARD

Faace! Fey, is dear a brogue upon my faash too? 70

ARCHER

Upon my soulvation, dere ish, joy. – But cussen Mackshane, vil you not put a remembrance upon me?

FOIGARD

(*Aside*) Mackshane! By St Paatrick, dat is naame, shure enough.

AIMWELL

I fancy, Archer, you have it.

FOIGARD

The devil hang you, joy. – By fat acquaintance are you my 75
cussen?

ARCHER

O, de devil hang yourshelf, joy, you know we were little boys togeder upon de school, and your foster moder's son was married upon my nurse's chister, joy, and so we are Irish cussens. 80

FOIGARD

De devil taak the relation! Vel, joy, and fat school was it?

ARCHER

I tinks it vas – aay – 'twas Tipperary.

66–7 *Mynheer . . . sacramant* 'Sir, I don't know what you are saying, I don't understand you indeed'. Foigard attempts to speak Flemish to prove he was born in Brussels.
82 *Tipperary* 'a free grammar school, founded in 1669' (Cordner)

FOIGARD

No, no, joy, it vas Kilkenny.

AIMWELL

That's enough for us. – Self-confession. – Come, sir, we must
deliver you into the hands of the next magistrate.   85

ARCHER

He sends you to gaol, you're tried next assizes, and away you go
swing into purgatory.

FOIGARD

And is it so with you, cussen?

ARCHER

It vil be sho wid you, cussen, if you don't immediately confess
the secret between you and Mrs Gipsy. – Look ye, sir, the   90
gallows or the secret, take your choice.

FOIGARD

The gallows! Upon my shoul I hate that saam gallow, for it is a
diseash dat is fatal to our family. – Vel den, dere is nothing,
shentlemens, but Mrs Sullen would spaak wid the count in her
chamber at midnight, and dere is no haarm, joy, for I am to   95
conduct the count to the plash, myshelf.

ARCHER

As I guessed. – Have you communicated this matter to the
count?

FOIGARD

I have not sheen him since.

ARCHER

Right again. Why then, doctor, – you shall conduct me to the   100
lady instead of the count.

FOIGARD

Fat, my cussen to the lady! Upon my shoul, gra, dat is too much
upon the brogue.

ARCHER

Come, come, doctor, consider we have got a rope about your
neck, and if you offer to squeak, we'll stop your windpipe,   105

---

83 *Kilkenny* 'the Protestant college of St John at Kilkenny; Swift and Congreve were among
the students educated there' (Cordner).

85 *magistrate* He would be handed over to the local magistrate, and held in gaol until the
next 'assizes' (l. 86), the court presided over by a judge of the high court which dealt with
serious criminal offences and those subject to capital punishment. The penalty for trea-
son was of course death: 'go swing in purgatory' (l. 86–7).

most certainly; we shall have another job for you in a day or
two, I hope.

AIMWELL

Here's company coming this way, let's into my chamber, and
there concert our affair further.

ARCHER

Come, my dear cussen, come along.   110

Exeunt

Enter BONNIFACE, HOUNSLOW *and* BAGSHOT *at one door,*
GIBBET *at the opposite*

GIBBET

Well, gentlemen, 'tis a fine night for our enterprise.

HOUNSLOW

Dark as hell.

BAGSHOT

And blows like the devil. Our landlord here has showed us the
window where we must break in, and tells us the plate stands in
the wainscoat cupboard in the parlour.   115

BONNIFACE

Ay, ay, Mr Bagshot, as the saying is, knives and forks, and cups,
and cans, and tumblers, and tankards. – There's one tankard,
as the saying is, that's near upon as big as me, it was a present to
the squire from his godmother, and smells of nutmeg and
toast like an East India ship.   120

HOUNSLOW

Then you say we must divide at the stair-hcad?

BONNIFACE

Yes, Mr Hounslow, as the saying is. – At one end of that gallery
lies my Lady Bountiful and her daughter, and at the other, Mrs
Sullen. – As for the squire –

GIBBET

He's safe enough, I have fairly entered him, and he's more   125
than half-seas over already. – But such a parcel of scoundrels

117 *cans* metal drinking vessels
119–20 *smells . . . toast* referring to the practice of putting pieces of toast sprinkled with
    sugar and nutmeg or other spices into wine
125 *entered him* started him drinking; for this military metaphor, compare III.iii.256–7.
126 *half-seas over* half drunk

99

are got about him now, that, egad, I was ashamed to be seen in
their company.

BONNIFACE

'Tis now twelve, as the saying is. – Gentlemen, you must set out
at one.   130

GIBBET

Hounslow, do you and Bagshot see our arms fixed, and I'll
come to you presently.

HOUNSLOW ⎱ We will.   *Exeunt*
BAGSHOT   ⎰

GIBBET

Well, my dear Bonny, you assure me that Scrub is a coward.

BONNIFACE

A chicken, as the saying is. – You'll have no creature to deal with   135
but the ladies.

GIBBET

And I can assure you, friend, there's a great deal of address
and good manners in robbing a lady. I am the most a gentleman
that way that ever travelled the road. – But, my dear Bonny, this
prize will be a galleon, a Vigo business. – I warrant you we   140
shall bring off three or four thousand pound.

BONNIFACE

In plate, jewels, and money, as the saying is, you may.

GIBBET

Why then, Tyburn, I defy thee. I'll get up to town, sell off my
horse and arms, buy myself some pretty employment in the
household, and be as snug, and as honest as any courtier of   145
'um all.

BONNIFACE

And what think you then of my daughter Cherry for a wife?

GIBBET

Look ye, my dear Bonny – Cherry *is the goddess I adore*, as the
song goes. But it is a maxim that man and wife should never

137–9 *there's. . . . the road* For Gibbet's claims see the note at V.ii.127–30.
140 *Vigo business* In 1702 ships loaded with treasure from the New World were captured by
     a combined British and Dutch fleet under Sir George Rooke off Vigo on the north-west
     coast of Spain.
143 *Tyburn* site of public executions in London (near the present Marble Arch)
145 *household* i.e. the royal household. Places in the household like commissions in the
     services could be bought.

have it in their power to hang one another, for if they should,   150
the Lord have mercy on 'um both.

Exeunt

ACT V. [SCENE i]

Scene continues

Knocking without: Enter BONNIFACE

BONNIFACE

Coming, coming. – A coach and six foaming horses at this time
o'night! Some great man, as the saying is, for he scorns to travel
with other people.

Enter SIR CHARLES FREEMAN

SIR CHARLES

What, fellow! A public-house, and a-bed when other people
sleep.   5

BONNIFACE

Sir, I an't a-bed, as the saying is.

SIR CHARLES

Is Mr Sullen's family a-bed, think ye?

BONNIFACE

All but the squire himself, sir, as the saying is, he's in the house.

SIR CHARLES

What company has he?

BONNIFACE

Why, sir, there's the constable, Mr Gage the exciseman, the   10
hunchbacked barber, and two or three other gentlemen.

SIR CHARLES

I find my sister's letters gave me the true picture of her spouse.

Enter SULLEN *drunk*

151 Q concludes: *End of the Fourth Act*
  0 s.d. 1 *Scene continues* the inn
 10 *exciseman* customs officer; during the wars with France large quantities of French goods
    were smuggled into the country. See Kenny I, 483–4.

BONNIFACE

Sir, here's the squire.

SULLEN

The puppies left me asleep. – Sir.

SIR CHARLES

Well, sir? 15

SULLEN

Sir, I'm an unfortunate man. – I have three thousand pound a year, and I can't get a man to drink a cup of ale with me.

SIR CHARLES

That's very hard.

SULLEN

Ay, sir. – And unless you have pity upon me, and smoke one pipe with me, I must e'en go home to my wife, and I had rather 20 go to the devil by half.

SIR CHARLES

But, I presume, sir, you won't see your wife tonight, she'll be gone to bed – you don't use to lie with your wife in that pickle?

SULLEN

What! Not lie with my wife! Why, sir, do you take me for an 25 atheist, or a rake?

SIR CHARLES

If you hate her, sir, I think you had better lie from her.

SULLEN

I think so too, friend – but I'm a justice of peace, and must do nothing against the law.

SIR CHARLES

Law! As I take it, Mr Justice, nobody observes law for law's sake, 30 only for the good of those for whom it was made.

SULLEN

But if the law orders me to send you to gaol, you must lie there, my friend.

SIR CHARLES

Not unless I commit a crime to deserve it.

SULLEN

A crime! Oons, an't I married? 35

21 *to* ed. (not in Q)
32 *gaol* ed. (goal Q)

SIR CHARLES

Nay, sir, if you call marriage a crime, you must disown it for a law.

SULLEN

Eh! – I must be acquainted with you, sir. – But, sir, I should be very glad to know the truth of this matter.

SIR CHARLES

Truth, sir, is a profound sea, and few there be that dare wade   40
deep enough to find out the bottom on't. Besides, sir, I'm afraid the line of your understanding mayn't be long enough.

SULLEN

Look ye, sir, I have nothing to say to your sea of truth, but if a good parcel of land can entitle a man to a little truth, I have as much as any he in the country.   45

BONNIFACE

I never heard your worship, as the saying is, talk so much before.

SULLEN

Because I never met with a man that I liked before.

BONNIFACE

Pray, sir, as the saying is, let me ask you one question: are not man and wife one flesh?   50

SIR CHARLES

You and your wife, Mr Guts, may be one flesh, because ye are nothing else; – but rational creatures have minds that must be united.

SULLEN

Minds?

---

42 *line* referring figuratively to a line to take soundings in water

51-3 *one flesh . . . united* Larson cites the following to illustrate how close Sir Charles's philosophy of marriage is to Milton's: 'the solace and satisfaction of the mind is regarded and provided for before the sensitive pleasing of the body' (*Prose Works*, II, 246); 'This is that rational burning that marriage is to remedy' (*Prose Works*, II, 251); 'what can be a fouler incongruity, a greater violence to the reverend secret of nature, than to force a mixture of minds that cannot unite' (*Prose Works*, II, 270); 'Marriage is a human society . . . if the mind, therefore, cannot have due company by marriage that it may reasonably and humanly desire that marriage can be no human society' (*Prose Works*, II, 275); 'the greatest breach [of marriage] . . . unfitness of mind' (*Prose Works*, II, 276); 'the unity of mind is nearer and greater than the union of bodies' (*Prose Works*, II, 606).

SIR CHARLES
Ay, minds, sir. Don't you think that the mind takes place of the   55
body?
SULLEN
In some people.
SIR CHARLES
Then the interest of the master must be consulted before that of
his servant.
SULLEN
Sir, you shall dine with me tomorrow. – Oons, I always thought   60
we were naturally one.
SIR CHARLES
Sir, I know that my two hands are naturally one, because they love
one another, kiss one another, help one another in all the actions
of life, but I could not say so much if they were always at cuffs.
SULLEN
Then 'tis plain that we are two.   65
SIR CHARLES
Why don't you part with her, sir?
SULLEN
Will you take her, sir?
SIR CHARLES
With all my heart.
SULLEN
You shall have her tomorrow morning, and a venison pasty into
the bargain.   70
SIR CHARLES
You'll let me have her fortune too?
SULLEN
Fortune! Why I have no quarrel at her fortune – I only hate the
woman, sir, and none but the woman shall go.
SIR CHARLES
But her fortune, sir –
SULLEN
Can you play at whisk, sir?   75
SIR CHARLES
No, truly, sir.

---

55 *takes place of* takes precedence of, goes before, an obsolete sense; see *OED* 'place' 27 c
64 *at cuffs* fighting
75 *whisk* See the note at I.i.80.

SULLEN

Nor at all-fours?

SIR CHARLES

Neither.

SULLEN

[*Aside*] Oons! Where was this man bred? – Burn me, sir, I can't
go home, 'tis but two a clock.   80

SIR CHARLES

For half an hour, sir if you please. But you must consider 'tis
late.

SULLEN

Late! That's the reason I can't go to bed. – Come, sir.

Exeunt

Enter CHERRY, *runs across the stage and knocks at* AIMWELL'*s
chamber door.
Enter* AIMWELL *in his night-cap and gown*

AIMWELL

What's the matter? You tremble, child, you're frighted.

CHERRY

No wonder, sir. – But in short, sir, this very minute a gang of   85
rogues are gone to rob my Lady Bountiful's house.

AIMWELL

How!

CHERRY

I dogged 'em to the very door, and left 'em breaking in.

AIMWELL

Have you alarmed anybody else with the news?

CHERRY

No, no, sir, I wanted to have discovered the whole plot, and   90
twenty other things to your man, Martin, but I have searched
the whole house and can't find him. Where is he?

AIMWELL

No matter, child. Will you guide me immediately to the house?

CHERRY

With all my heart, sir. My lady Bountiful is my godmother, and I
love Mrs Dorinda so well –   95

77 *all-fours* a card game for two players, 'like whist, it was a rural or servants' pastime'
(Kenny)

AIMWELL

Dorinda! The name inspires me, the glory and the danger shall be all my own. – Come, my life, let me but get my sword.

Exeunt

[ACT V. SCENE ii]

Scene changes to a bedchamber in LADY BOUNTIFUL's *house*

Enter MRS SULLEN, DORINDA, *undressed, a table and lights*

DORINDA

'Tis very late, sister. No news of your spouse yet?

MRS SULLEN

No, I am condemned to be alone till towards four, and then, perhaps I may be executed with his company.

DORINDA

Well, my dear, I'll leave you to your rest. You'll go directly to bed, I suppose?   5

MRS SULLEN

I don't know what to do. Heigh-ho!

DORINDA

That's a desiring sigh, sister.

MRS SULLEN

This is a languishing hour, sister.

DORINDA

And might prove a critical minute, if the pretty fellow were here.

MRS SULLEN

Here! What, in my bedchamber at two a clock o'th'morning, I   10
undressed, the family asleep, my hated husband abroad, and my lovely fellow at my feet – O gad, sister!

---

0 s.d. 2 *undressed* not naked, of course, but the opposite of '*dressed*' (II.i.0 s.d.2): not dressed to appear in public

3 *executed* playing on *condemned* in her previous phrase

6 *Heigh-ho* a 'desiring sigh', as Dorinda says, and the kind Beatrice affects in *Much Ado*: 'I may sit in a corner and cry "Heigh-ho for a husband!" ' (II.i.350)

8 *languishing* suffering 'amorous languor', see *OED* 'languisher'; a heroine in Sheridan's *The Rivals* is Lydia Languish.

11 *family* meaning not her relatives but the whole household

DORINDA

Thoughts are free, sister, and them I allow you. – So, my dear, good night.

MRS SULLEN

A good rest to my dear Dorinda.   15

[*Exit* DORINDA]

Thoughts free! Are they so? Why then suppose him here, dressed like a youthful, gay and burning bridegroom, (*Here* ARCHER *steals out of the closet*) with tongue enchanting, eyes bewitching, knees imploring. (*Turns a little o' one side, and sees* ARCHER *in the posture she describes*) Ah! (*Shrieks, and runs to the*   20 *other side of the stage*) Have my thoughts raised a spirit? – What are you, sir, a man or a devil?

ARCHER

A man, a man, madam.   *Rising*

MRS SULLEN

How shall I be sure of it?

ARCHER

Madam, I'll give you demonstration this minute.   25

Takes her hand

MRS SULLEN

What, sir! Do you intend to be rude?

ARCHER

Yes, madam, if you please.

MRS SULLEN

In the name of wonder, whence came ye?

ARCHER

From the skies, madam. – I'm a Jupiter in love, and you shall be my Alcmena.   30

---

26 *rude* impolite, but with a sexual overtone; Compare this dialogue between Loveless and Amanda in Cibber's *Love's Last Shift* (16 Jan 1695/6): '*Lov.* . . . Come, now pull away your Hand to make me hold it faster. *Am.* Nay, now you are rude, Sir. *Lov.* If love be Rudeness, let me be Impudent: When we are familiar, Rudeness will be Love. No Woman ever thought a Lover rude, after she had once granted him the Favour.' (IV.iii.132–7). See *Colley Cibber: Three Sentimental Comedies* ed. Maureen Sullivan (New Haven 1973).

29–30 *Jupiter . . . Alcmena* Jupiter assumed the appearance of the husband, Amphitryon, to deceive his wife, Alcmena. Here the link is the sudden appearance of the lover, not his imitation of the husband. Plautus's *Amphitruo* is the classical Roman comedy version of the story, and Dryden's *Amphitryon* (1690) successfully modernized it.

30 *Alcmena* ed. (Alimena Q)

MRS SULLEN

How came you in?

ARCHER

I flew in at the window, madam, your cousin Cupid lent me his wings, and your sister Venus opened the casement.

MRS SULLEN

I am struck dumb with admiration.

ARCHER

And I with wonder.   *Looks passionately at her*   35

MRS SULLEN

What will become of me?

ARCHER

How beautiful she looks. – The teeming jolly spring smiles in her blooming face, and when she was conceived, her mother smelt to roses, looked on lilies.

Lilies unfold their white, their fragrant charms,   40
When the warm sun thus darts into their arms.
Runs to her

MRS SULLEN

Ah! (*Shrieks*)

ARCHER

Oons, madam, what d'ye mean? You'll raise the house.

MRS SULLEN

Sir, I'll wake the dead before I bear this. – What, approach me with the freedoms of a keeper! I'm glad on't, your impudence   45
has cured me.

ARCHER

(*Kneels*) If this be impudence, I leave to your partial self. No panting pilgrim after a tedious, painful voyage, e'er bowed before his saint with more devotion.

---

39 *smelt . . . lilies* referring to the belief that events or circumstances at the moment of conception could influence the child
smelt to the more frequent construction until the nineteenth century, when 'smell at' gradually replaced it. (*OED* smell, II. 6.a.)

40–41 *Lilies . . . arms* Like Aimwell in IV.i, Archer woos in verse.

45 *keeper* See the note at I.i.190.

47 *partial* kindly disposed, sympathetic (he hopes she is)

MRS SULLEN

> (*Aside*) Now, now, I'm ruined if he kneels. – Rise, thou prostrate   50
> engineer, not all thy undermining skill shall reach my heart. –
> Rise, and know, I am a woman without my sex, I can love to all
> the tenderness of wishes, sighs and tears – but go no further.
> Still to convince you that I'm more than woman, I can speak my
> frailty, confess my weakness even for you – but –   55

ARCHER

> For me!   *Going to lay hold on her*

MRS SULLEN

> Hold, sir, build not upon that – for my most mortal hatred
> follows if you disobey what I command you now: leave me this
> minute. (*Aside*) If he denies, I'm lost.

ARCHER

> Then you'll promise –   60

MRS SULLEN

> Anything another time.

ARCHER

> When shall I come?

MRS SULLEN

> Tomorrow, when you will.

ARCHER

> Your lips must seal the promise.

MRS SULLEN

> Pshaw!   65

ARCHER

> They must, they must. (*Kisses her*) Raptures and paradise! And
> why not now, my angel? The time, the place, silence and secrecy,
> all conspire. – And the now conscious stars have preordained
> this moment for my happiness.   *Takes her in his arms*

MRS SULLEN

> You will not, cannot, sure.   70

---

51 *engineer . . . undermining* terms from the military use of mines; compare the Prologue to
The Twin Rivals: 'Your critic-engineers safe underground, / Blow up our works, and all
our art confound.' (ll.17–18)

52 *without my sex* without inherent female frailty; compare l. 54: 'I'm more than woman'.
Fifer paraphrases: ' "beyond the capacity or comprehension of" my sex'.

68 *now conscious stars* Archer suggests the stars, normally unaware of human desires, have
ordained this moment for his happiness.

69 s.d. *Takes her in his arms* ed. (Takes her in her arms Q)

ARCHER

If the sun rides fast, and disappoints not mortals of tomorrow's
dawn, this night shall crown my joys.

MRS SULLEN

My sex's pride assist me.

ARCHER

My sex's strength help me.

MRS SULLEN

You shall kill me first.   75

ARCHER

I'll die with you.   *Carrying her off*

MRS SULLEN

Thieves, thieves, murder –

Enter SCRUB *in his breeches, and one shoe*

SCRUB

Thieves, thieves, murder, popery.

ARCHER

Ha! The very timorous stag will kill in rutting time.
                                        Draws and offers to stab SCRUB

SCRUB

(*Kneeling*) O, pray, sir, spare all I have and take my life.   80

MRS SULLEN

(*Holding* ARCHER'*s hand*) What does the fellow mean?

SCRUB

O, madam, down upon your knees, your marrow bones. –
He's one of 'em.

ARCHER

Of whom?

SCRUB

One of the rogues – I beg your pardon, sir, one of the honest   85
gentlemen that just now are broke into the house.

ARCHER

How?

---

76 *die with you* See the note at IV.i.392 for the sexual sense of 'die'.
82 *marrow bones* a humorous expression for knees

MRS SULLEN

I hope you did not come to rob me?

ARCHER

Indeed, I did, madam, but would have taken nothing but what
you might have spared, but your crying 'Thieves' has waked this 90
dreaming fool, and so he takes 'em for granted.

SCRUB

Granted! 'Tis granted, sir, take all we have.

MRS SULLEN

The fellow looks as if he were broke out of Bedlam.

SCRUB

Oons, madam, they're broke into the house with fire and sword,
I saw them, heard them, they'll be here this minute. 95

ARCHER

What, thieves?

SCRUB

Under favour, sir, I think so.

MRS SULLEN

What shall we do, sir?

ARCHER

Madam, I wish your ladyship a good night.

MRS SULLEN

Will you leave me? 100

ARCHER

Leave you! Lord, madam, did not you command me to be gone
just now upon pain of your immortal hatred.

MRS SULLEN

Nay, but pray, sir –   *Takes hold of him*

ARCHER

Ha, ha, ha, now comes my turn to be ravished. – You see now,
madam, you must use men one way or other. But take this by 105
the way, good madam, that none but a fool will give you the
benefit of his courage, unless you'll take his love along with it. –
How are they armed, friend?

SCRUB

With sword and pistol, sir.

---

93 *Bedlam* the Bethlem Hospital in London, until 1751 'England's only public madhouse'
(Roy Porter, *Disease, Medicine and Society in England, 1550–1860*, 2nd ed., (Basingstoke
1993) p. 22.)

ARCHER

Hush! – I see a dark lantern coming through the gallery. –   110
Madam, be assured I will protect you, or lose my life.

MRS SULLEN

Your life! No, sir, they can rob me of nothing that I value half so
much; therefore, now, sir, let me entreat you to be gone.

ARCHER

No, madam, I'll consult my own safety for the sake of yours;
I'll work by stratagem. Have you courage enough to stand the   115
appearance of 'em?

MRS SULLEN

Yes, yes, since I have scaped your hands, I can face anything.

ARCHER

Come hither brother Scrub, don't you know me?

SCRUB

Eh! My dear brother, let me kiss thee.   *Kisses* ARCHER

ARCHER

This way – here.   120

ARCHER and SCRUB *hide behind the bed*

Enter GIBBET *with a dark lantern in one hand and a pistol
in t'other*

GIBBET

Ay, ay, this is the chamber, and the lady alone.

MRS SULLEN

Who are you, sir? What would you have? D'ye come to rob me?

GIBBET

Rob you! Alack a day, madam, I'm only a younger brother,
madam, and so, madam, if you make a noise, I'll shoot you
through the head. But don't be afraid, madam. (*Laying his*   125
lantern and pistol upon the table) These rings, madam, don't be

---

110 *dark lantern* 'a lantern with a slide or arrangement by which the light can be concealed'
(*OED*) (lanthorn Q, the old spelling reflecting the fact that lanterns were originally
made of horn)
123 *younger brother* Gentlemanly Gibbet claims he is not a thief, but simply a younger
brother who has inherited nothing, and is therefore hard up.

concerned, madam, I have a profound respect for you, madam. Your keys, madam, don't be frighted, madam, I'm the most of a gentleman. (*Searching her pockets*) This necklace madam, I never was rude to a lady – I have a veneration – for this necklace – 130

> *Here* ARCHER *having come round and seized the pistol,*
> *takes* GIBBET *by the collar, trips up his heels, and claps*
> *the pistol to his breast*

ARCHER

Hold, profane villain, and take the reward of thy sacrilege.

GIBBET

Oh! Pray, sir, don't kill me, I an't prepared.

ARCHER

How many is there of 'em, Scrub?

SCRUB

Five and forty, sir. 135

ARCHER

Then I must kill the villain to have him out of the way.

GIBBET

Hold, hold, sir, we are but three upon my honour.

ARCHER

Scrub, will you undertake to secure him?

SCRUB

Not I, sir. Kill him, kill him.

ARCHER

Run to Gipsy's chamber, there you'll find the doctor. Bring him hither presently. 140

> *Exit* SCRUB *running*

Come, rogue, if you have a short prayer, say it.

127–30 *profound respect . . . veneration* Gibbet's language was matched by actual highwaymen who treated their victims with gentlemanly courtesy. See J. M. Beattie, *Crime and the Courts in England 1660–1800* (Princeton 1986), p.153, for reports of highwaymen 'being excessively polite, especially to women: not pointing their guns, returning some favoured object, not searching them.' Gibbet does of course search Mrs Sullen, in his boasted gentlemanly fashion, as well as remove the 'rings' and 'necklace' she is wearing.
131 s.d. 1 *pistol* ed., 1728 (pistols Q)
141 *presently* immediately

GIBBET

Sir, I have no prayer at all; the government has provided a chaplain to say prayers for us on these occasions.

MRS SULLEN

Pray, sir, don't kill him. – You fright me as much as him.   145

ARCHER

The dog shall die, madam, for being the occasion of my disappointment. – Sirrah, this moment is your last.

GIBBET

Sir, I'll give you two hundred pound to spare my life.

ARCHER

Have you no more, rascal?

GIBBET

Yes, sir, I can command four hundred, but I must reserve two   150
of 'em to save my life at the sessions.

Enter SCRUB *and* FOIGARD

ARCHER

Here, doctor, I suppose Scrub and you between you may manage him. – Lay hold of him, doctor.

FOIGARD *lays hold of* GIBBET

GIBBET

What, turned over to the priest already. – Look ye, doctor, you come before your time. I an't condemned yet, I thank ye.   155

FOIGARD

Come, my dear joy, I vill secure your body and your shoul too. I vill make you a good Catholic, and give you an absolution.

GIBBET

Absolution! Can you procure me a pardon, doctor?

FOIGARD

No, joy.   160

GIBBET

Then you and your absolution may go to the devil.

---

143 s.p. GIBBET Q2 (*Gip.* Q)
150–51 *reserve . . . sessions* By bribing the magistrates, he plans to ensure he is not sent to the assizes. Magistrates presided over the quarter sessions which dealt with less serious offences than the assizes. See the note at IV.ii.85.

ARCHER

Convey him into the cellar, there bind him. – Take the pistol, and if he offers to resist, shoot him through the head, – and come back to us with all the speed you can.

SCRUB

Ay, ay, come, doctor, do you hold him fast, and I'll guard   165
him.

MRS SULLEN

But how came the doctor?

ARCHER

In short, madam – (*Shrieking without*) S'death! The rogues are at work with the other ladies. – I'm vexed I parted with the pistol, but I must fly to their assistance. – Will you stay here,   170
madam, or venture yourself with me?

MRS SULLEN

O, with you, dear sir, with you.

Takes him by the arm and exeunt

[ACT V. SCENE iii]

Scene changes to another apartment in the same house

Enter BAGSHOT *dragging in* LADY BOUNTIFUL, *and* HOUNSLOW
hauling in DORINDA, *the rogues with swords drawn*

HOUNSLOW

Come, come, your jewels, mistress.

BAGSHOT

Your keys, your keys, old gentlewoman.

Enter AIMWELL *and* CHERRY

AIMWELL

Turn this way, villains. I durst engage an army in such a cause.

He engages 'em both

---

0 s.d. 2 BAGSHOT *dragging in . . . HOUNSLOW* ed. Q has the thieves' names reversed, but the dialogue, as Kenny points out (II, 230), makes it clear that Hounslow is holding Dorinda, and Bagshot Lady Bountiful.

DORINDA

   O, madam, had I but a sword to help the brave man!

LADY BOUNTIFUL

   There's three or four hanging up in the hall, but they won't   5
   draw. I'll go fetch one, however.   *Exit*

Enter ARCHER *and* MRS SULLEN

ARCHER

   Hold, hold, my lord, every man his bird, pray.
     They engage man to man; the rogues are thrown and disarmed

CHERRY

   [*Aside*] What, the rogues taken! Then they'll impeach my father.
   I must give him timely notice.   *Runs out*

ARCHER

   Shall we kill the rogues?   10

AIMWELL

   No, no, we'll bind them.

ARCHER

   (*To* MRS SULLEN *who stands by him*) Ay, ay; here, madam, lend
   me your garter?

MRS SULLEN

   The devil's in this fellow. He fights, loves, and banters, all in a
   breath. – Here's a cord that the rogues brought with 'em, I   15
   suppose.

ARCHER

   Right, right, the rogue's destiny, a rope to hang himself. – Come,
   my lord – this is but a scandalous sort of an office (*Binding the*
   rogues together) if our adventures should end in this sort of
   hangman work. But I hope there is something in prospect that –   20

Enter SCRUB

   Well, Scrub, have you secured your Tartar?

SCRUB

   Yes, sir, I left the priest and him disputing about religion.

---

  7 *bird* as if they are out shooting
 21 *Tartar* thieves' slang for a thief, a beggar (here, meaning Gibbet)

AIMWELL

And pray carry these gentlemen to reap the benefit of the controversy.

Delivers the prisoners to SCRUB *who leads them out*

MRS SULLEN

Pray, sister, how came my lord here?   25

DORINDA

And pray, how came the gentleman here?

MRS SULLEN

I'll tell you the greatest piece of villainy –

They talk in dumb-show

AIMWELL

I fancy, Archer, you have been more successful in your adventures than the house-breakers.

ARCHER

No matter for my adventure, yours is the principal. – Press her   30
this minute to marry you, – now while she's hurried between
the palpitation of her fear, and the joy of her deliverance, now
while the tide of her spirits are at high flood. – Throw yourself
at her feet, speak some romantic nonsense or other. – Address
her like Alexander in the height of his victory, confound her   35
senses, bear down her reason, and away with her. – The Priest is
now in the cellar, and dare not refuse to do the work.

Enter LADY BOUNTIFUL

AIMWELL

But how shall I get off without being observed?

ARCHER

You a lover and not find a way to get off! – Let me see.

AIMWELL

You bleed, Archer.   40

ARCHER

S'death, I'm glad on't; this wound will do the business. – I'll

35 *Alexander* Another reference to the general of ancient Greece, and also to the popular
stage presentation of him in *The Rival Queens* (see the note at IV.i.263); hence Archer can
refer to the style of his speeches.
38 *get off* get away (with Dorinda)

amuse the old lady and Mrs Sullen about dressing my wound while you carry off Dorinda.

LADY BOUNTIFUL

Gentlemen, could we understand how you would be gratified for the services –   45

ARCHER

Come, come, my lady, this is not time for compliments, I'm wounded, madam

LADY BOUNTIFUL ⎱
MRS SULLEN ⎰ How! Wounded!

DORINDA

I hope, sir, you have received no hurt?

AIMWELL

None but what you may cure.   *Makes love in dumb-show*   50

LADY BOUNTIFUL

Let me see your arm, sir. – I must have some powder-sugar to stop the blood. – O me, an ugly gash, upon my word, sir! You must go into bed.

ARCHER

Ay, my lady, a bed would do very well. – (*To* MRS SULLEN) Madam, will you do me the favour to conduct me to a chamber?   55

LADY BOUNTIFUL

Do, do, daughter – whilst I get the lint and the probe and the plaster ready.

          Runs out one way, AIMWELL *carries off* DORINDA *another*

ARCHER

Come, madam, why don't you obey your mother's commands?

MRS SULLEN

How can you, after what is past, have the confidence to ask me?

ARCHER

And if you go to that, how can you, after what is past, have the   60
confidence to deny me? – Was not this blood shed in your defence, and my life exposed for your protection? – Look ye, madam, I'm none of your romantic fools, that fight giants and monsters for nothing; my valour is downright Swiss. I'm a soldier of fortune and must be paid.   65

64 *Swiss* referring to the mercenaries employed as guards by various European monarchs

MRS SULLEN

'Tis ungenerous in you, sir, to upbraid me with your services.

ARCHER

'Tis ungenerous in you, madam, not to reward 'em.

MRS SULLEN

How, at the expense of my honour!

ARCHER

Honour! Can honour consist with ingratitude? If you would
deal like a woman of honour, do like a man of honour: d'ye   70
think I would deny you in such a case?

Enter a SERVANT

SERVANT

Madam, my lady ordered me to tell you that your brother is
below at the gate.   [*Exit*]

MRS SULLEN

My brother! Heavens be praised. – Sir, he shall thank you for
your services; he has it in his power.   75

ARCHER

Who is your brother, madam?

MRS SULLEN

Sir Charles Freeman. – You'll excuse me, sir; I must go and
receive him.   [*Exit*]

ARCHER

Sir Charles Freeman! S'death and hell! – My old acquaintance.
Now unless Aimwell has made good use of his time, all our fair   80
machine goes souse into the sea like the Eddystone.   *Exit*

---

81 *souse* splash; 'souse' here meaning 'the act of plunging into water' (*OED*)
   Eddystone the first lighthouse marking the Eddystone Rocks off Plymouth, completed in
   1698, was destroyed by a hurricane in 1703

[ACT V. SCENE iv]

Scene changes to the gallery in the same house

Enter AIMWELL *and* DORINDA

DORINDA

Well, well, my lord, you have conquered. Your late generous
action will, I hope, plead for my easy yielding, though I must
own your lordship had a friend in the fort before.

AIMWELL

The sweets of Hybla dwell upon her tongue. – Here, doctor –

Enter FOIGARD *with a book*

FOIGARD

Are you prepared boat?   5

DORINDA

I'm ready. But, first, my lord, one word. – I have a frightful
example of a hasty marriage in my own family; when I reflect
upon't, it shocks me. Pray, my lord, consider a little –

AIMWELL

Consider! Do you doubt my honour or my love?

DORINDA

Neither. I do believe you equally just as brave. – And were your   10
whole sex drawn out for me to choose, I should not cast a look
upon the multitude if you were absent. – But my lord, I'm a
woman: colours, concealments may hide a thousand faults in
me. – Therefore know me better first; I hardly dare affirm I
know myself in anything except my love.   15

AIMWELL

(*Aside*) Such goodness who could injure? I find myself unequal
to the task of villain. She has gained my soul, and made it
honest like her own. – I cannot, cannot hurt her. – Doctor,
retire.

Exit FOIGARD

2 *plead . . . yielding* excuse my having accepted you so easily
4 *Hybla* a town in Sicily famous from antiquity for fine honey
13 *colours* outward appearances

Madam, behold your lover and your proselyte, and judge of my   20
passion by my conversion. – I'm all a lie, nor dare I give a fiction
to your arms. I'm all counterfeit except my passion.

DORINDA

Forbid it Heaven! A counterfeit!

AIMWELL

I am no lord, but a poor needy man, come with a mean, a
scandalous design to prey upon your fortune. – But the beauties   25
of your mind and person have so won me from myself, that, like
a trusty servant, I prefer the interest of my mistress to my own.

DORINDA

Sure I have had a dream of some poor mariner, a sleepy image
of a welcome port, and wake involved in storms. – Pray, sir, who
are you?   30

AIMWELL

Brother to the man whose title I usurped, but stranger to his
honour or his fortune.

DORINDA

Matchless honesty. – Once I was proud, sir, of your wealth and
title, but now am prouder that you want it: now I can show my
love was justly levelled, and had no aim but love. Doctor, come   35
in.

Enter FOIGARD *at one door,* GIPSY *at another, who whispers*
to DORINDA

Your pardon, sir, we shan't want you now, sir. You must excuse
me. – I'll wait on you presently.

Exit with GIPSY

FOIGARD

Upon my shoul, now, dis is foolish.   *Exit*

AIMWELL

Gone, and bid the priest depart. – It has an ominous look.   40

Enter ARCHER

20 *proselyte* convert
34 *want* lack
37 *shan't want you now* ed. (shannot; won't you now Q)

ARCHER

Courage, Tom! – Shall I wish you joy?

AIMWELL

No.

ARCHER

Oons, man, what ha' you been doing?

AIMWELL

O, Archer, my honesty, I fear, has ruined me.

ARCHER

How?   45

AIMWELL

I have discovered myself.

ARCHER

Discovered, and without my consent! What, have I embarked my small remains in the same bottom with yours, and you dispose of all without my partnership?

AIMWELL

O, Archer, I own my fault.   50

ARCHER

After conviction. – 'Tis then too late for pardon. – You may remember, Mr Aimwell, that you proposed this folly. – As you begun it, so end it. – Henceforth I'll hunt my fortune single. – So farewell.

AIMWELL

Stay, my dear Archer, but a minute.   55

ARCHER

Stay! What, to be despised, exposed and laughed at? – No, I would sooner change conditions with the worst of the rogues we just now bound than bear one scornful smile from the proud knight that once I treated as my equal.

AIMWELL

What knight?   60

ARCHER

Sir Charles Freeman, brother to the lady that I had almost – but no matter for that, 'tis a cursed night's work, and so I leave you to make your best on't.   *Going*

48 *bottom* ship, boat
52 *proposed* ed. (poposed Q)

AIMWELL

Freeman! – One word, Archer. Still I have hopes; methought she
received my confession with pleasure.   65

ARCHER

S'death, who doubts it?

AIMWELL

She consented after to the match, and still I dare believe she will
be just.

ARCHER

To herself, I warrant her, as you should have been.

AIMWELL

By all my hopes, she comes, and smiling comes.   70

Enter DORINDA *mighty gay*

DORINDA

Come, my dear lord – I fly with impatience to your arms. – The
minutes of my absence was a tedious year. Where's this tedious
priest?

Enter FOIGARD

ARCHER

Oons, a brave girl.

DORINDA

I suppose, my lord, this gentleman is privy to our affairs?   75

ARCHER

Yes, yes, madam. I'm to be your father.

DORINDA

Come, priest, do your office.

ARCHER

Make haste, make haste, couple 'em any way. (*Takes* AIMWELL's
hand) Come, madam, I'm to give you –

DORINDA

My mind's altered, I won't.   80

ARCHER

Eh!

72–3 *tedious . . . tedious priest* Q (tedious . . . this priest 1728). The repetition is probably a
printer's error.

AIMWELL

I'm confounded.

FOIGARD

Upon my shoul, and sho is myshelf.

ARCHER

What's the matter now, madam?

DORINDA

Look ye, sir, one generous action deserves another. – This   85
gentleman's honour obliged him to hide nothing from me; my
justice engages me to conceal nothing from him. In short, sir,
you are the person that you thought you counterfeited. You are
the true Lord Viscount Aimwell, and I wish your lordship joy.
Now, priest, you may be gone. If my lord is pleased now with   90
the match, let his lordship marry me in the face of the world.

AIMWELL ⎫
        ⎬ What does she mean?
ARCHER ⎭

DORINDA

Here's a witness for my truth.

Enter SIR CHARLES *and* MRS SULLEN

SIR CHARLES

My dear Lord Aimwell, I wish you joy.

AIMWELL

Of what?   95

SIR CHARLES

Of your honour and estate. Your brother died the day before I
left London, and all your friends have writ after you to Brussels.
Among the rest, I did myself the honour.

ARCHER

Hark ye, sir knight, don't you banter now?

SIR CHARLES

'Tis truth, upon my honour.   100

AIMWELL

Thanks to the pregnant stars that formed this accident.

ARCHER

Thanks to the womb of time that brought it forth. Away with it!

101 *pregnant* fruitful, filled with momentous results

AIMWELL

Thanks to my guardian angel that led me to the prize.

Taking DORINDA's *hand*

ARCHER

And double thanks to the noble Sir Charles Freeman. My lord,
I wish you joy. My lady, I wish you joy. – Egad, Sir Charles,   105
you're the honestest fellow living. – S'death, I'm grown strange
airy upon this matter. – My lord, how d'ye? – A word, my lord;
don't you remember something of a previous agreement that
entitles me to the moiety of this lady's fortune, which, I think,
will amount to five thousand pound?   110

AIMWELL

Not a penny, Archer. You would ha' cut my throat just now,
because I would not deceive the lady.

ARCHER

Ay, and I'll cut your throat again, if you should deceive her now.

AIMWELL

That's what I expected, and to end the dispute, the lady's
fortune is ten thousand pound. We'll divide stakes. Take the ten   115
thousand pound, or the lady.

DORINDA

How! Is your lordship so indifferent?

ARCHER

No, no, no, madam, his lordship knows very well that I'll take
the money. I leave you to his lordship, and so we're both
provided for.   120

Enter COUNT BELLAIR

COUNT

Mesdames, et Messieurs, I am your servant trice humble. I hear
you be rob here.

---

105 *Charles* ed. (Freeman Q) a probable printer's error, 'Freeman' catching the eye two lines
   above, instead of *Charles*; Archer might be expected to address his friend in the correct
   form, the title followed by the given name. Myers, however, retains 'Freeman', suggest-
   ing 'the solecism may be a piece of insolence' from Archer.
107 *airy* 'lively, sprightly, merry, gay, vivacious' (*OED*); a quality dear to Farquhar's heart
   and at the centre of his imagined admirable man about town, and incorporated into his
   name: Sir Harry Wildair in *The Constant Couple* and *Sir Harry Wildair*.
109 *moiety* half

AIMWELL

The ladies have been in some danger, sir.

COUNT

And begar, our inn be rob too.

AIMWELL

Our inn! By whom? 125

COUNT

By the landlord, begar. – Garzoon, he has rob himself and run away.

ARCHER

Robbed himself!

COUNT

Ay, begar, and me too of a hundre pound.

ARCHER

A hundred pound? 130

COUNT

Yes, that I owed him.

AIMWELL

Our money's gone, Frank.

ARCHER

Rot the money, my wench is gone. – *Savez vous quelque chose de Mademoiselle* Cherry?

Enter a fellow with a strong box and a letter

FELLOW

Is there one Martin here? 135

ARCHER

Ay, ay, – who wants him?

FELLOW

I have a box here and letter for him.

ARCHER

(*Taking the box*) Ha, ha, ha, what's here? Legerdemain? By this light, my lord, our money again. But this unfolds the riddle. (*Opening the letter, reads*) Hum, hum, hum – O, 'tis for the 140 public good, and must be communicated to the company.

133–4 *Savez . . . de* Do you know anything about
138 *Legerdemain* slight of hand, conjuring tricks

Mr Martin,
My father being afraid of an impeachment by the rogues that
are taken tonight is gone off, but if you can procure him a
pardon he will make great discoveries that may be useful to   145
the country. Could I have met you instead of your master
tonight, I would have delivered myself into your hands with
a sum that much exceeds that in your strong box, which I
have sent you, with an assurance to my dear Martin, that
I shall ever be his most faithful friend till death.   150

CHERRY BONNIFACE

There's a billet-doux for you. – As for the father, I think he
ought to be encouraged, and for the daughter, pray, my lord,
persuade your bride to take her into her service instead of
Gipsy.   155

AIMWELL

I can assure you, madam, your deliverance was owing to her
discovery.

DORINDA

Your command, my lord, will do without the obligation. I'll
take care of her.

SIR CHARLES

This good company meets opportunely in favour of a design   160
I have in behalf of my unfortunate sister. I intend to part her
from her husband. – Gentlemen, will you assist me?

ARCHER

Assist you! S'death, who would not?

COUNT

Assist! Garzoon, we all assist.

Enter SULLEN

SULLEN

What's all this? – They tell me, spouse, that you had like to have   165
been robbed?

MRS SULLEN

Truly, spouse, I was pretty near it – had not these two gentlemen
interposed.

152 *billet-doux* love-letter

SULLEN

How came these gentlemen here?

MRS SULLEN

That's his way of returning thanks, you must know. 170

COUNT

Garzoon, the question be apropos for all dat.

SIR CHARLES

You promised last night, sir, that you would deliver your lady to me this morning.

SULLEN

Humph.

ARCHER

Humph. What do you mean by humph? – Sir, you shall deliver 175
her. – In short, sir, we have saved you and your family, and if you are not civil we'll unbind the rogues, join with 'em and set fire to your house. – What does the man mean? Not part with his wife!

COUNT

Ay, garzoon, de man no understan common justice. 180

MRS SULLEN

Hold, gentlemen, all things here must move by consent, compulsion would spoil us. Let my dear and I talk the matter over, and you shall judge it between us.

SULLEN

Let me know first who are to be our judges. – Pray, sir, who are you? 185

SIR CHARLES FREEMAN

I am Sir Charles Freeman, come to take away your wife.

SULLEN

And you, good sir?

AIMWELL

Charles, Viscount Aimwell, come to take away your sister.

SULLEN

And you pray, sir?

ARCHER

Francis Archer, Esq., come – 190

---

171 *apropos* relevant, to the purpose

188 *Charles, Viscount Aimwell* As Jeffares notes, Archer elsewhere calls him Tom, e.g. II.ii.16, 35, 40; III.ii.1. This may be another printer's error, *Charles* being repeated from two lines above.

SULLEN

To take away my mother, I hope. – Gentlemen, you're heartily welcome, I never met with three more obliging people since I was born. – And now, my dear, if you please, you shall have the first word.

ARCHER

And the last, for five pound.   195

MRS SULLEN

Spouse.

SULLEN

Rib.

MRS SULLEN

How long have we been married?

SULLEN

By the Almanac, fourteen months. – But by my account, fourteen years.   200

MRS SULLEN

'Tis thereabout by my reckoning.

COUNT

Garzoon, their account will agree.

MRS SULLEN

Pray, spouse, what did you marry for?

SULLEN

To get an heir to my estate.

SIR CHARLES

And have you succeeded?   205

SULLEN

No.

ARCHER

The condition fails of his side. – Pray, madam, what did you marry for?

MRS SULLEN

To support the weakness of my sex by the strength of his, and to enjoy the pleasures of an agreeable society.   210

SIR CHARLES

Are your expectations answered?

197 *Rib* wife, because Eve was created from Adam's rib (Genesis 2. 22)
207 *The condition . . . side* His intentions in marrying have been disappointed.
209 *weakness of my sex* another reference by Mrs Sullen to the conventional notion of women as weaker vessels, inherently inferior to men physically and emotionally; compare V.ii.52.

MRS SULLEN
　No.
COUNT
　A clear case, a clear case.
SIR CHARLES
　What are the bars to your mutual contentment?
MRS SULLEN
　In the first place, I can't drink ale with him.　　　　　　　　215
SULLEN
　Nor can I drink tea with her.
MRS SULLEN
　I can't hunt with you.
SULLEN
　Nor can I dance with you.
MRS SULLEN
　I hate cocking and racing.
SULLEN
　And I abhor ombre and piquet.　　　　　　　　　　　　　220
MRS SULLEN
　Your silence is intolerable.
SULLEN
　Your prating is worse.
MRS SULLEN
　Have we not been a perpetual offence to each other – a gnawing
　vulture at the heart?
SULLEN
　A frightful goblin to the sight.　　　　　　　　　　　　　225
MRS SULLEN
　A porcupine to the feeling.
SULLEN
　Perpetual wormwood to the taste.
MRS SULLEN
　Is there on earth a thing we could agree in?
SULLEN
　Yes – to part.

219　*cocking* cock-fighting
220　*ombre and piquet* fashionable card games
227　*wormwood* bitter tasting herb (*artemisia absinthium*) used for various domestic and
　　medicinal preparations

MRS SULLEN
   With all my heart.   230

SULLEN
   Your hand.

MRS SULLEN
   Here.

SULLEN
   These hands joined us, these shall part us – away –

MRS SULLEN
   North.

SULLEN
   South.   235

MRS SULLEN
   East.

SULLEN
   West – far as the poles asunder.

COUNT
   Begar, the ceremony be vera pretty.

SIR CHARLES
   Now, Mr Sullen, there wants only my sister's fortune to make us
   easy.   240

SULLEN
   Sir Charles, you love your sister, and I love her fortune,
   everyone to his fancy.

ARCHER
   Then you won't refund?

SULLEN
   Not a stiver.

ARCHER
   Then I find, madam, you must e'en go to your prison again.   245

COUNT
   What is the portion?

SIR CHARLES
   Ten thousand pound, sir.

COUNT
   Garzoon, I'll pay it, and she shall go home wid me.

---

244 *Not a stiver* Nothing, Not a penny. A stiver was a small Dutch coin of low value.

ARCHER

Ha, ha, ha, French all over. – Do you know, sir, what ten
thousand pound English is?   250

COUNT

No, begar, not justement.

ARCHER

Why, sir, 'tis a hundred thousand livres.

COUNT

A hundre tousan livres! – A garzoon, me canno do't, your
beauties and their fortunes are both too much for me.

ARCHER

Then I will. – This night's adventure has proved strangely lucky   255
to us all. – For captain Gibbet in his walk had made bold,
Mr Sullen, with your study and escritoire, and had taken out
all the writings of your estate, all the articles of marriage with
your lady, bills, bonds, leases, receipts to an infinite value. I
took 'em from him, and I deliver them to Sir Charles.   260

                    Gives him a parcel of papers and parchments

SULLEN

How, my writings! My head aches consumedly. – Well,
gentlemen, you shall have her fortune, but I can't talk. If you
have a mind, Sir Charles, to be merry, and celebrate my sister's
wedding, and my divorce, you may command my house – but
my head aches consumedly. – Scrub, bring me a dram.   265

ARCHER

(*To* MRS SULLEN) Madam, there's a country dance to the trifle
that I sung today; your hand, and we'll lead it up.

                                        Here a dance

'Twould be hard to guess which of these parties is the better
pleased, the couple joined, or the couple parted, the one
rejoicing in hopes of an untasted happiness, and the other in   270
their deliverance from an experienced misery.

---

251 *justement* exactly (French)
252 *livres* an old French coin worth a tenth of a pound sterling; As Myers notes (p. xvi), it is
     inconceivable that the Count would not know the value of this coin.
257 *escritoire* writing desk
259 *your Comedies*, second edition [1711], Kenny (his Q, Cordner)

Both happy in their several states we find,
Those parted by consent, and those conjoined.
Consent, if mutual, saves the lawyer's fee,
Consent is law enough to set you free. 275

274 *Consent* The basis of Milton's notion of divorce; Larson quotes 'then is there no power above their own consent to hinder them from unjoining' (*Prose Works*, II, 328); 'Not he who puts away by mutual consent [commits adultery]' (*Prose Works*, II, 669); see also: 'it is a less breach of wedlock to part with wise and quiet consent betimes, than still to soil and profane that mystery and joy of union with a polluting sadness and perpetual distemper' (*Prose Works*, II, 258).

AN EPILOGUE

DESIGNED TO BE SPOKE IN THE BEAUX' STRATAGEM

If to our play your judgment can't be kind,
Let its expiring author pity find.
Survey his mournful case with melting eyes,
Nor let the bard be damned before he dies.
Forbear you fair on his last scene to frown,   5
But his true exit with a plaudit crown.
Then shall the dying poet cease to fear
The dreadful knell, while your applause he hears.
At Leuctra so the conquering Theban died,
Claimed his friends' praises, but their tears denied: 10
Pleased in the pangs of death he greatly thought
Conquest with loss of life but cheaply bought.
The difference this, the Greek was one would fight
As brave, though not so gay as Sergeant Kite.
Ye sons of Will's, what's that to those who write?   15
To Thebes alone the Grecian owed his bays,
You may the bard above the hero raise,
Since yours is greater than Athenian praise.

Designed ... stratagem A 1730 duodecimo edition of the play published by Lintott identifies the author for the first time: 'By Mr Smith, the Author of *Phaedra and Hippolytus*'. Edmund Smith's play opened at the same theatre as Farquhar's, the Queen's, six weeks later, on 21 April 1707.

2 *expiring author* Farquhar died two months after the play was first performed.

9 *Leuctra* The Thebans defeated the Spartans at Leuctra in 371 BC. Their leader, Epaminondas was not, as Smith has it, killed then, but died nine years later in a further battle with the Spartans at Mantinea.

14 *Kite* the Sergeant in Farquhar's *The Recruiting Officer*. Witty, ingenious and outrageous, 'gay', in Farquhar's word, Kite is one of his greatest comic roles.

15 *sons of Will's* the writers who patronized this coffee-house; see also III.ii.81.

16 *bays* the wreath of bay leaves awarded to the victorious soldier, or poet

APPENDIX

MODIFICATIONS TO THE ROLE OF COUNT BELLAIR

A note at III.iii.287 in the sixth edition of Farquhar's *Works* (1728) is the first evidence of the suppression of the role of the Count: 'This scene printed in *italic*, with the entire part of the *Count*, was cut out by the Author, after the first Night's representation; and where he shou'd enter in the last scene of the fifth Act, it is added to the Part of *Foigard*.' The eight changes made in V.iv to incorporate the French Count's lines in the part of the Irish Foigard appear as follows in the *Works* (1728):

l. 121

Enter FOIGARD

FOIGARD
Arrah, fait, de people do say you be all robbed, joy.
AIMWELL
The ladies have been in some danger, sir, as you saw.
FOIGARD
Upon my shoul, our inn be rob too.
AIMWELL
Our inn! By whom?
FOIGARD
Upon my shalvation, our landlord has robbed himself and run away wid da money.
ARCHER
Robbed himself!
FOIGARD
Ay, fait, and me too of a hundre pound.
ARCHER
Robbed you of a hundred pound!
FOIGARD
Yes, fait, honey, that I did owe to him.

l. 164

FOIGARD

Ay, upon my shoul, we'll all asshist.

l. 171

FOIGARD

Ay, but upon my conshience, de question be apropos for all dat.

l. 180

FOIGARD

Arrah, not part wid your wife! Upon my shoul, de man dosh not understand common shivility.

l. 202

FOIGARD

Upon my conshience, dere accounts vil agree.

l. 213

FOIGARD

Arrah, honey, a clear caase, a clear caase.

l. 238

FOIGARD

Upon my shoul, a very pretty sheremony.

ll. 246–8

ARCHER

What is her portion?

SIR CHARLES

Ten thousand pound, sir.

ARCHER

I'll pay it. My lord, I thank him, has enabled me, and, if the lady pleases, she shall go home with me. This night's adventure . . .

(Continues as Q; ll. 249–55 'Ha, ha, ha . . . will' not in 1728)

9 780713 670004